Part I | Neo-Classicism to Pop

Late 18th & 19th
Century Textiles

Neo-Classicism to Pop

Part I | Late 18th & 19th Century Textiles

by Sue Kerry

Francesca Galloway
in association with
the Antique Collectors' Club

To coincide with
the exhibition
5th-28th September 2007
Francesca Galloway
31 Dover Street
London W1S 4ND
t: 0207 499 6844
f: 0207 491 1684

First published in 2007
by Francesca Galloway in association with the
Antique Collectors' Club

Francesca Galloway
francesca@francescagalloway.com
www.francescagalloway.com

Antique Collectors' Club
Sandy Lane, Old Martlesham Woodbridge,
Suffolk, IP12 4SD, UK
Eastworks, 116 Pleasant Street - Suite 18
Easthampton, MA 01027, USA

Text: © Francesca Galloway
and Sue Kerry
Images: © Francesca Galloway

ISBN 978 185149 555 9

Edited by Julie Pickard
Designed by Anikst Design
Photography by Matt Pia

Printed in Italy

Contents

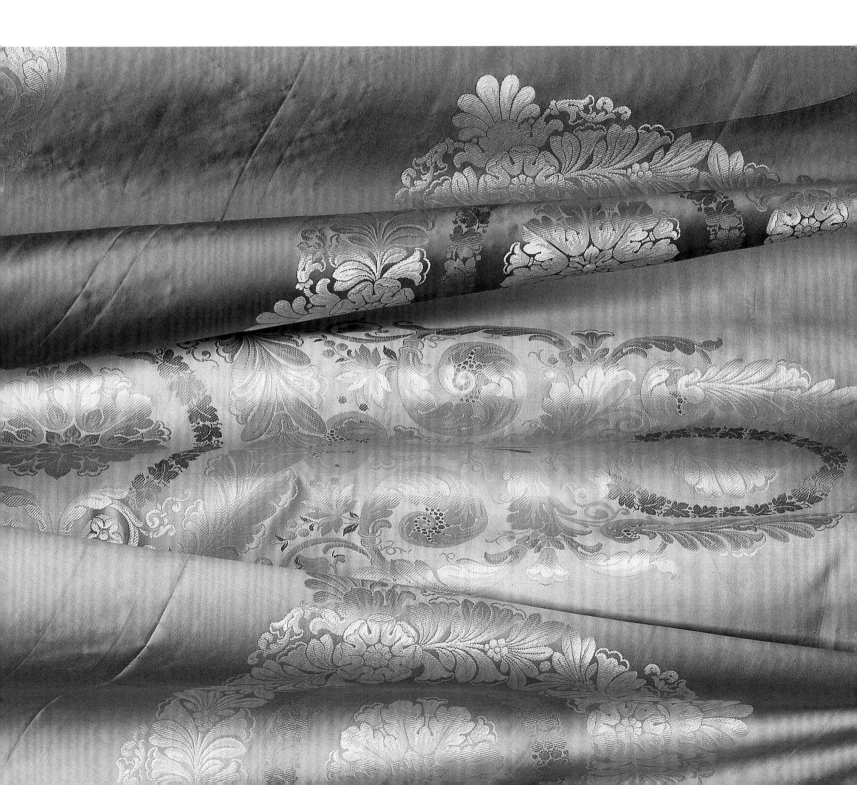

Acknowledgements

We would like to thank the following people without whose help this publication would not have been possible: Mary Schoeser, Lesley Miller, John Gregory, Zöe Hendon, Maggie Smith, Audrey Mathieu, Maria-Anne Privat-Savigny, Isabel Bretones, Anna Jolly, Florence Charpigny, Isabelle Tamisier-Vétois, Arnauld Berjon de Lavergnée, Robert Hughes, Marie-Noëlle Sudre, Stephane Degraeuwe, Xavier Petticol, Aude Leveau-Falgayrettes, Pamela Goblin, Philippe Verzier, Mavis Kerry, Anne Forray-Carlier, Jean-Paul LeClercq, Odile Nouvel, Catherine Join-Dieterle, Dominique Fabre, Patrick Lelievre, Helen Sydney, Ann Grafton, Philip Sykas, Howard Coutts, Eleanor Tollfee, Jenny Lister, Kitty Morris, Janie Lightfoot, Helen Loveday, Debbie Williams, Julie Pickard, Alison Docherty, Avodica Ash.

In particular we are indebted to Misha Anikst, Matt Pia, Christine Ramphal and Rukmani Rathore.

Francesca Galloway
Sue Kerry

Introduction

Neo-Classical

The Lyon silk industry was established during the early sixteenth century when King François I (1494–1547) granted two Piedmontese silk merchants, Estienne Turquet and Paule Nariz, the right to set up a silk weaving workshop. The aim of the royal decree was to encourage domestic manufacture, which would compete effectively with silk imports from Italy. By the late seventeenth century French weaving enterprises had grown and prospered to such an extent that silks from Lyon, Paris and Tours were considered among the best of their kind in Europe. Around 1665 the industry engaged 80,000 workers. Louis XIV (1638–1715) took a great interest in the sericulture and silk weaving of Lyon through his prime minister, Jean-Baptiste Colbert. The latter achieved a reputation for his work in improving French manufacturing and for bringing the economy back from the brink of bankruptcy. Colbert issued many edicts in order to ensure a high quality of silk production, with penalties for those who did not follow the rules. If a merchant was found to have unsatisfactory cloth on three concurrent occasions he was to be tied to a tree with the offending cloth attached to him. Louis patronised those workshops which were of an exceptional standard. In 1666 the Lyon silk industry provided the Royal Court with substantial quantities of not only plain fabrics but also complicated figured patterns. Most important in regulating high standards was the Royal Decree of 1667 in which new rules were laid down for the *Grande Fabrique*, the name used for the silk-weaving guild of Lyon, an organisation comprising many small workshops. This guild was to ensure that a high quality of weaving was maintained so that the reputation of Lyon was held in high regard throughout Europe. It also ensured protection for the weavers attached to the *Grande Fabrique* from inferior weavers or inexperienced craftsmen who were not part of the guild. These craftsmen were unable to obtain orders from the Royal Court, because the Royal Court guaranteed to purchase only from those weavers belonging to the *Grande Fabrique*. The *Garde-Meuble*, the department of the King's household that ordered and cared for the interior decoration and maintenance of the royal residences, ordered directly from the *Grande Fabrique*. The two establishments were closely linked for political, economic and social reasons, the royal palaces acting as a showplace for French silks. If there was an economic decline, war, famine, social unrest or the greater threat of foreign imports – such as the fashion at the time for painted silk from China or chintzes from India – then the French silk weavers suffered, as did the country. They often petitioned the Crown for help, and the *Garde-Meuble* responded by placing orders to redecorate various royal palaces, including the Palace of Versailles, for example, during 1726–1730.

From 1756 to 1785, a succession of wars took its toll on France, from the Seven Years' War (1756–63) to France's involvement in the American War of Independence (1778–

Cat. 2

83). A further blight to the trade was the import of foreign textiles. In the second half of the century embroidered and printed fabric rather than woven silk became fashionable, thus threatening the livelihood of the silk weavers. Due to political and economic pressures the *Garde-Meuble* could not order as many woven silks as the weavers had hoped. In the late 1780s, however, under the jurisdiction of Thierry de Ville d'Avray, the *Garde-Meuble* played a key role in boosting the *Grande Fabrique,* investing heavily in Lyonnais silk production, now one of the finest in Europe. From 1785 to 1789, Thierry de Ville d'Avray began the process of stocking and redecorating the palaces of Saint Cloud, Rambouillet and Compiègne for the court of Louis XVI (1754–1793), thus enabling Lyonnais silk manufacturers to re-open their workshops. Silks were woven not only for furniture but also for curtains, wall coverings, bed hangings and screen upholstery, as well as ornamental bordering for walls or curtain drapes. The scale of the order was impressive because each room had two sets of furnishings, one for winter and another for summer. Consequently the orders provided the boost that Lyonnais weavers needed.

It was not uncommon for weavers to re-weave existing designs for several equally prestigious clients; to do this meant that the weaver saved on the costs of new preparatory work such as design and technical loom adjustments. Neo-Classical silk lampas (**cat no 1b**) is typical of the designs woven by many Lyonnais firms and is the style of design for which Lyon became famous as the eighteenth century closed. Often a small selection of designs was varied by introducing only small alterations to the original design. In the case of our silk lampas, the design was modified by the change of the deer and unicorn motifs, or an alteration to the laurel trail pediment. Such silk cloths were woven on draw-looms, which required an extra worker to operate the pattern-making mechanism, which was attached to the loom. The draw boy made sure that the right warp threads were lifted in the correct sequence, in order for the weft threads to be distributed to produce the pattern. Oral tradition among silk weavers suggests that the draw-loom produced flaws due to human error; for example, the sheds of the warp might stick and the weft become misaligned. In contrast, in the nineteenth century, new mechanical weaving equipment produced a regular and unspoilt ground cloth or, alternately, a consistently repeated flaw. Most master craftsmen, however, could produce flawless cloth whether on a draw-loom or a mechanical loom. The minute and irregular flaws in our silk indicate that it was made from a draw-loom. In style, it closely resembles the documented silks by the silk-manufacturing firm of Reboul et Fontebrune of Lyon, from around 1785 to 1793.

In the summer of 1789 one of the most powerful monarchies in Europe was overthrown by revolutionaries who favoured constitutional rule. Ten years of political turmoil followed as moderate parliamentarians and radical republicans fought over the political future of France. Lyon was besieged and looted in 1793, causing many of the workshops to close down and manufacturing records to be lost. Royal palaces were loot-

Cat. 1b

ed, furniture was burnt so as to recover the gold and silver required to pay for ammunition, other items were exported and sold, and the new régime, the *Directoire* (1795-99), delved into the reserves of the *Garde-Meuble* to decorate their own residences in a manner they felt they deserved.

The political unrest and the many different ideals represented by the French Revolution were impossible to reconcile and a new era of authoritarian rule began in 1799 under the dashing revolutionary general, Napoleon Bonaparte (1769-1821). The Lyonnais region at this time experienced high unemployment, a shortage of raw silk and a mass migration of weavers from Lyon to England, Switzerland and Italy. A handful even journeyed as far as the United States, contributing to that nation's nascent silk industry. Such drastic actions caused difficulties for the *Grande Fabrique*, which was now forced to train new weavers, harness-makers, throwsters and designers. In addition, it now had to sustain itself in the face of fierce competition from other European silk-weaving centres that had benefited from the migration of the Lyon weavers.

By 1800, the results of other fundamental changes were also being felt. In the previous half century, many design schools had been set up to cater for the needs of luxury trades such as silk weaving. Many started by teaching figure drawing as the basis of design, but by the 1760s new schools focused purely on the drawing of ornament and flowers. Designers often combined formal training in the classroom with hands-on experience in manufacturing workshops. This combination of artistic and technical experience produced new and dramatic designs in the new and classical taste. Today these designs would be described as 'show stoppers'. At the same time, the designers also had the ability to produce small-figured silks, which would be produced *en masse* and sold as a 'core line' through a pattern agency or manufacturer. Many designers were now highly trained in both drawing and in the technology of weaving, and they worked closely with the weavers to ensure that the design was executed as they had imagined. The weavers were often members of small established family units, who had woven a particular cloth type for generations; they worked independently, receiving contracts for weaving from silk merchants based in their locality. In a few exceptional circumstances the silk merchants would own their own weaving sheds, employing approximately five to twenty weavers, of which, often, two or three were master weavers (i.e. fully trained and qualified), with the rest being journeymen or apprentices. The journeymen weavers sometimes moved from region to region working for different silk merchants and as their skill progressed so did their ability to weave more difficult cloths and thus attract higher pay.

This catalogue includes fabrics from the distinguished Lyonnais weaver, Camille Pernon (1753–1808). Examination of his life shows his resolve, good fortune and entrepreneurial fortitude. Camille Pernon was of the youngest generation of a silk-weaving

Cat. 5

dynasty based on the outskirts of Lyon, at Sainte-Foy-lès-Lyon. The firm was entrusted with weaving cloth for the Royal Court, supplying cloth to the *Garde-Meuble* from 1780 until 1793. Pernon was lucky that in the year 1792–93 he was able to supply the final piece of a substantial order just before the *Grande Fabrique* suspended all production. Pernon had previously survived economic depressions that had befallen Lyon by turning his hand to horse trading, dealing in Arabian horses from North Africa. He also had a deep fascination with science and had the idea of producing a light aircraft (which bore similarities to an aircraft glider), but due to the poor economy, funding was non-existent and thus the project was never realised. He did, however, have a brief scientific success when he and the wallpaper magnate of Paris, Jean-Baptiste Réveillon, funded the attempt by the brothers Joseph and Jacques-Étienne Montgolfier to fly the first hot air balloon in 1783. The balloon consisted of a silk taffeta that was varnished with alum. Pernon possibly supplied the silk which made the Montgolfiers' balloon. Pernon also used what little reserves of silk yarn he had as equity and funded a Parisian bank, gaining stock interest and thus wealth. (Such an action was not uncommon, for silk yarn was at certain times worth more than currency. Consequently several silk weaving firms throughout Europe supported monetary operations such as banks.) From this brief account it can be surmised that he had developed a wide network of contacts who could have helped him through his difficult times, and in this way he was able to keep the firm and himself afloat.

However, due to the patronage of the aristocracy and his success in weaving luxurious cloth for the court and the wealthiest members of society, he was an enemy of the new Republic. He fled France to Genoa in Italy, escaping the guillotine. From there he went to London. His success in England is not known, but he did take out an advertisement in *The Times* in 1794, offering his services as one 'Monsieur Camille Pernon - designer, silk weaver, harness maker'. He was propitiously based in St Stephens, Spitalfields, then the source of Britain's finest silks. It is possible that he was also simply sourcing future work in Britain for his firm, as he had done previously in Russia at the Royal Court of Catherine the Great. Having spent the year 1783 working on the redecoration of her palaces in and around St Petersburg, Pernon received the title of *Agent of Her Imperial Majesty of All the Russias*. After the Revolution, Pernon returned to Lyon in 1795 and began to rebuild his business. From 1797 to 1799 he received a prestigious order from the Spanish Royal Court, manufacturing silk designs by Jean-Démosthène Dugourc, who had been commissioned to design the silken ensemble for the interior of the Palace of Aranjuez, near Madrid. Dugourc and Pernon had previously worked together in 1781. Dugourc, son of the Comptroller to the Duc d'Orléans, had spent his childhood in privileged surroundings. Trained as an engraver, he subsequently worked in many other decorative art disciplines. The crown recognised his talents, making him in 1784

Cat. 3

Dessinateur de la Garde-Meuble. His work for the French court had been restrained, but his work for the Spanish Court was grandiose and thoroughly original.

Since the mid-eighteenth century there had emerged a shift in taste to that of the Neo-Classical style, replete with floral urns, swathes of ribbons and threads of pearls or arabesques with mythological elements. Designs were symmetrical, and would often be very large and long in their design repeat. Distinguished decorative artists such as Dugourc were often trained at the technical schools, which were based in Lyon or Paris. They included accomplished flower painters and all were keenly aware of the fashionable tastes of the time. Sadly, little information survives as to who many of these designer-draughtsmen were. Even the now-anonymous men provided an essential service, working on commissions for the manufacturers to the Royal Court, whether they were making tapestries (Gobelins), carpets (Savonnerie), or weaving the most elaborate and costly furnishing silks, as the wholesaler merchant Cartier or the weaver Camille Pernon did.

Pernon wove fabric for the Spanish Court from 1799 until 1808, including silk cloth for the dressing room of the Queen of Spain. The two Neo-Classical panels illustrated in this catalogue (**cat no 4**) are linked stylistically to those he made for the Casita del Labrador at Aranjuez. The composition is the same and the centre pieces, which are separate, depict what is assumed to be scenes from the Aranjuez estate. The weaver produced the panels with a plain silk in the centre cameo sections. The embroiderer would then have supplied a scene which was specified by the client. This manufacturing method shows that the same 'outline' design could be woven for several clients, becoming unique only by the change of the scenic centre panel. These panels were intended for a billiard room. As in the case of most wall hangings, the silks would have been stretched onto wooden strips before being fastened to the walls. The cloth, which was of a luxurious quality, would have produced a grand effect upon the wall, not only from the result of the intricate design, but also from the sheen of the satin areas, which are densely woven. Additionally the cloth's innate thermal properties kept the room's interior warm in winter, whilst keeping it cool in summer.

Cat. 4

Cat. 4

Empire

By the start of the nineteenth century the Lyon silk industry once again received help from those in power. The new consul, Napoleon Bonaparte, like previous royal patrons before him, began to place commissions in order to revive the silk industry of Lyon. Napoleon (who was barely thirty years old) was declared the first consul or *Premier Consul de facto* in 1799. For the next fourteen years he blazed across Europe and parts of Russia, conquering country after country and fighting war after war, both on land and at sea. The first three years of his rule saw the Revolution's democratic aspirations smothered as he ruthlessly centralised France under his sole power. Once France was firmly under his control, in 1804, he declared himself Emperor. To the workers of Lyon, Napoleon was a saviour. In 1802, wishing to revive the plundered silk industry and wanting to restore his palaces to their once-glorious state, he placed orders with Lyonnais silk firms, boosting the flagging industry and ensuring that the silk trade would be successful for many years to come. He visited the town on several occasions, first to rally support for himself and subsequently to show that he wanted to revive the town's industry. By 1804 the list of residences to be refurbished not only included Fontainebleau, the Tuileries, Saint Cloud and Versailles, but also extended beyond the former frontiers of France to include the Pitti Palace in Florence, the Laeken Palace in Belguim, the Rohan estate in Strasbourg and the Monte Cavallo (during the nineteenth century its name was changed to the Quirinal Palace) in Rome, as well as numerous campaign tents. All were bedecked in Lyonnais silks that honoured the status and stature of this man.

Designs for silks during this period were much simpler and more refined. The ornate Neo-Classical style gave way to a simpler classicism, sourced directly from antiquity. Medallions, rosettes and palmettes were used alongside laurel and olive leaves, myrtle, and oak and scrolling acanthus leaves; the use of such motifs was laden with symbolic meaning. In antiquity, laurel or an olive leaf crown was given to the winner at the ancient Olympic Games, and remained a symbol for peace and victory. Oak continued to be a symbol for hospitality, stability, strength and liberty; it also had a connotation of 'saviour', since it was believed that Jesus Christ's cross had been made from oak. The eagle represented courage, faith, generosity and contemplation, and was therefore appropriate for military purposes. To use such meaningful motifs deliberately was not uncommon among emperors or kings, for it told visiting dignitaries that the state was powerful, grand and enduring. Britain likewise used emblems or motifs denoting its power as an empire, and in each case such motifs aimed to project an established and unopposed empire.

Thus the cloths for the state apartments serving Napoleon's new regime and empire conveyed a 'new' country that had strength and power. Silk cloths bore one or more of

Cat. 55

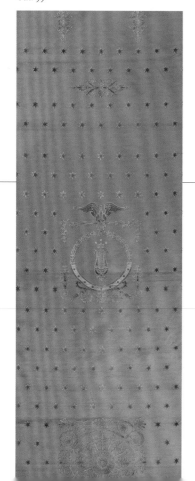

Cat. 6

these symbolic elements, including the letter initial 'N' from his name or the imperial eagle, the badge of state. Two examples are illustrated here. The silk (**cat no 55**) depicts the imperial eagle and the sceptre of state, and was originally woven in 1802–05 for the King of Naples (Napoleon's brother Joseph) as well as for use within the palace at Compiègne. A border of laurel leaves adorned the edge of a green silk damask and was used in the library of Napoleon Bonaparte at the Palace of Saint Cloud (**cat no 6**). Other examples woven for noble or aristocratic clients, and inspired by the fashion led by Napoleon, also show the use of imagery from antiquity. The piece *Lyre et Coupe* (Lyre and Goblet) (**cat no 9**) depicts a lyre and other motifs from antiquity and is surrounded by an ogival trail of leaves. The piece featuring two centurion helmets (**cat no 12**), conveys an imperial, Roman element. Such designs were produced by state artists or architects such as Pierre Percier and Charles Fontaine or the architect Alexandre Brogniart. The intention was that the cloth would act subliminally as propaganda for Napoleon's cause. Napoleon took a keen interest in the activities of the *Garde-Meuble*; he wished to know all. Regarding the furnishings he wrote '...it is important to choose good design and handsome models that avoid variations in the current fashion and that will last as long as possible' (Martin, R. (1983), p. 11). For the men in charge at the *Garde-Meuble*, life was difficult; not only did they have to respect imperial administrative and financial regulations, but they had also to serve a master whose requirements were legion and from whom no detail escaped. It is said that Napoleon complained that the architects and designers sacrificed comfort and ease of use to decorative opulence.

With many state buildings and palaces now to weave for, there began a new era of prosperity for the silk weavers of Lyon. Between 1804 and 1808, Camille Pernon was the foremost silk weaver in Lyon, having a few years earlier supplied the textile refurbishment of Saint Cloud. Pernon, along with the firm Cartier et Fils (a Parisian silk merchant), was given the exclusive right to provide cloth to the *Garde-Meuble* for the palaces of Saint Cloud, Fontainebleau, Laeken, Meudon and Compiègne. Then, in February 1806, Napoleon took the decision to refurbish Versailles and monies from the Emperor's estate were to be made available to provide cloth that equalled the quality and grandeur of the silks in other palaces which Napoleon claimed as his residences. Even though Napoleon never intended to live in Versailles, it still had to convey opulence. Pernon started to weave a crimson silk intended for the throne room, but the order was abandoned due to the redirection of money to finance the battle of Austerlitz and the Treaty at Tilsit in 1807.

Pernon suffered from the withdrawal of the order for Versailles, as well as from other changes to weaving orders and delays. Adding to his firm's problems, in 1808, the last year of his life, he lost his exclusive right to such work. Napoleon enabled twenty-four merchants and manufacturers who belonged to the *Grande Fabrique* to manufac-

Cat. 9

Cat. 12

ture for the *Garde-Meuble Impérial*, the imperial title for the *Garde-Meuble*. These manufacturers included Bissardon, Cousin et Bony, Boulard, Lacostat, Trollier and Grand Frères (successor to Pernon), and were the only firms at the time considered able to match the quality that had been established by Camille Pernon. Support from Napoleon continued. In 1810, he further examined the supply of goods from Lyon, and suggested that the French navy should purchase goods from the north and pay for it in silk fabrics from Lyon. He further helped the silk trade by insisting that silk goods exported to the United States should be sold at half their cost, with a subsidy to compensate for this 'loss-leader' activity. On 20 December 1810, Napoleon also made available two million francs to the Lyonnais industry, when he commissioned approximately 80,000 metres of plain and figured silk for the *Garde-Meuble*. Some of this silk was intended for the palaces of Versailles, Elysée and Monte Cavallo. Accounts show that 79,000 metres of silk was delivered by December 1813, of which 68,000 metres ultimately remained in storage at the *Garde-Meuble*.

Napoleon's attention to detail extended to the raw materials used in silk manufacture, and in 1808 he created a scientific institution to investigate dyes. This was partly the result of the bad experience with Pernon's weaving of green and poppy red (ponceau) silks for Saint Cloud. The silks had faded due to a defective mordant in the dye, and as such the vibrant red silk border became a delicate pink colour (**cat no 6**). The oversight tarnished Pernon's reputation, Napoleon commented that 'Foreigners who see modern furnishings in such condition cannot fail to have a very bad impression of the Lyonnais manufacturers' (Dumonthier, E. (1909a), p. 14). In 1810 Napoleon made a decree promoting research that would lead to an alternative blue to that of indigo. This dyestuff was imported from India and had become expensive due to insurrection shortages and war. The research prize of 25,000 francs went to a dye made from Prussian blue, although ironically this dye was not as lightfast as indigo. As a consequence of fading fabrics the *Garde-Meuble* brought in strict rulings for the supply and quality of silks. The *Garde-Meuble* checked the cloth for its stability and fugitiveness. The troublesome green was improved and eventually became the imperial colour, because Napoleon found it restful to the eye.

Included here is an example of a silk with this improved 'fast' green, featuring star shapes and rosettes (**cat no 7 & 8b**). It would have been used for the inner lining to curtains and bed hangings. The rosette silk, together with chair seat silks, also included in the catalogue, were the sort of designs that could be re-woven for other patrons and as a consequence the manufacturers took any opportunity to supply such silks to other clients. Indeed, in order to sustain work, manufacturers would take the opportunity to re-weave imperial designs by adapting the designs: they altered sections or produced very similar designs for wealthy patrons throughout France, Europe and the United

Cat. 7

Cat. 8b

States. In some cases, the designs which were woven exclusively for the Emperor could also be pirated by weavers who were not part of the *Grande Fabrique*, or by other European firms, who offered them to their own prestigious clients. A damask fabric woven by Pernon in 1805 for the palace of Saint Cloud, saw the image being pirated in c1816 and woven for the Prince Regent (later King George IV) by Messrs Wilson & Wood of, London.

Considering the drive to boost a flagging silk industry and his personal interest in his surroundings, what is all the more remarkable is how little time Napoleon Bonaparte had to enjoy the luxurious interiors he created. He spent twenty-eight months at Saint Cloud, little more than ten months at the Tuileries, five months at Fontainebleau, two months at the Elysée and five days at Laeken, while the palaces of Pitti and Monte Cavallo never received an imperial visit. Yet all were decorated substantially between 1802 and 1815. They left a significant legacy for the future: an easily identifiable aesthetic and also many unused silks in the imperial storerooms.

Restauration

As Napoleon was defeated in 1814 and sent into exile, the magnificent commissions which generated such prosperity for the Lyonnais silk industry suddenly stopped; weavers complained and feared another decline. The *Grande Fabrique* pressed the *Garde-Meuble* for more orders but to no avail. The reserves of the *Garde-Meuble* were already full from Napoleon's previous commissions and were thus available for his successors to use. Political events also precluded projects from being initiated or even completed. In many cases the fabrics stored at the *Garde-Meuble* were unusable due to imperial emblems that had been woven into them. Grand Frères was forced to weave insert pieces of silk so that alterations – to conceal the imperial bees, initial N, the imperial eagle and the crosses of the Legion of Honour – could be made to the fabrics stored at the *Garde-Meuble*.

Louis XVIII (1755–1824), aware of the decline in this important French industry, decided to restore and refurbish some of the royal residences. The programme started with the Tuileries, where he chose to reside. He decided on a dramatic transformation of the King's bed chamber, which Napoleon had previously abandoned in favour of the Throne Room. The cloth – a blue brocaded silk velvet featuring royal symbols and floral elements was the 'feature' cloth with a silk lining to the drapes in white similar to those

Cat. 19b

featured in a green colourway in this catalogue (cat no 19b). The curtain drapes were installed on the bed in July 1819, and King Louis died in this bed in September 1824. During the reign of Charles X (1757–1836) the bed was changed but the hangings were re-used upon a newly designed bed. In 1820 Grand Frères began to supply cloth for the Throne Room; the new layout was opulent and designed by Jean-Démosthène Duguorc, who in 1816 was reappointed as architect Royale to the Garde-Meuble. These orders for the Tuileries spawned many variations of fabric patterns by different manufacturers in Lyon. The decor featured royal shields, crowns, sceptres, fleur-de-lys and Holy crosses; designs were classical in taste as well as featuring floral elements that bore a resemblance to eighteenth-century styles, making a pointed visual reference to the Restauration. Cloths woven for Charles X include Marguerites, Roses and Tulips (cat no 16), designed by Jacques-Louis de la Hamayde de Saint-Ange, designer to the Garde-Meuble during the Restauration era, whose designs offered a lighter less formal design for the Court.

Such new commissions allowed more firms to tender for the honour of weaving, and manufacturers such as Chuard, Dutillieu, and Corderier et Lemire to produce cloth for the Royal residences. However, Royal orders under the Restauration period were dramatically reduced in number compared with the Empire period. Seeking alternative patrons, the *Grande Fabrique* found new clients among aristocrats, the bourgeois and rich Europeans, among them Jacob Mayer Rothschild, the Comte de Saint Simon, the Marquess of Londonderry, the Duke and Duchess of Devonshire, Prince Torlonia of Rome, the Duchess of Hamilton and the British Prince Regent. These people represented a mixture of established fortunes and those who had accrued their wealth through industry, trade and finance. They could afford luxury and comfort and were openly fashion-conscious in their living standards, not just in their personal dress. Original patterns were provided or designs previously woven for Royal palaces were re-woven for slightly less grand homes. As wars and uprisings began to cease, the wealthy classes began to restore old mansions or build new and even grander places to reside in, thus providing the Lyonnais silk manufacturers with orders for floral patterned fabrics or Neo-Classical designs. The diversity of both cloths and clients is the reason why fabrics from this time, such as the blue suite of furnishings (cat no 18) or the red silk chair and sofa coverings (cat no 14), cannot be identified with precision. Silks were logged with a manufacturer number plus client (patron) number, but over time associated order books and accounts have been lost, leaving it virtually impossible to identify who the patrons were. In many cases the weaver had used such codes specifically to protect the identity of their client; these could also include a pricing gauge and in some situations these still remain a secret today. Few people in the firm would know what these codes meant; this was to ensure that industrial espionage did not take place and, in particular, to defend against foreign competition, which was still a growing threat.

Cat. 16

Cat. 18

Technical advances in weaving and dyes included the use of the Jacquard loom invented in 1801 by Joseph Marie Jacquard, from an earlier adaptation by Jacques Vaucanson. The jacquard gradually replaced the draw-loom during the nineteenth century; however, there are known instances where some firms still used the draw-loom within their premises. Further development of dyes saw them becoming more stable and less expensive than imported natural dyes. Stronger resilient silk threads were produced through new and improved silk throwing methods. The advancement of loom adjustments and the use of the fly shuttle helped the weavers to produce significant amounts of cloth for these new private clients. Other fabric production techniques used in satisfying the demand for sumptuously furnished apartments included stencilling onto a 'finished' silk, which gave it strength and a wax effect look. This can be seen here on the stencilled silk canopy (**cat no 17**), which was most probably used for the inner canopy lining of a bed.

Fabric designs from both the Empire and Restauration periods witnessed a re-birth during the twentieth century, most notably those used by the successors to Grand Frères, Tassinari et Chatel, when they supplied silks during the 1960s for important interiors such as those in the White House (**cat no 10**).

As the Restauration period progressed the Neo-Classical style returned, and designs became an amalgam of Empire features, such as medallions or rosettes, with Greek urns and lyres from antiquity. Measurements of the designs show that their scale became slightly smaller, which can be seen in the yellow chair seat cover (**cat no 15**). With previous design styles there was a distinct *horror vacui*, with patterns covering all of the surface area of the furniture; whereas now, the fashion was for more of the ground cloth to be exposed. This type of cloth was also appropriate for the intimately scaled furniture of the period.

Political and social unrest arose again during the 1830s, disrupting the work of the *Grande Fabrique*. Charles X had proclaimed a law of the Divine Right of Kings, restoring the primogeniture and strict religious laws that were in accordance with the Catholic Church. He lowered interest rates on bonds so as to reimburse the émigrés who had lost land and property during the Revolution. These actions enraged the merchant classes and liberals who had become financially hurt by such actions, and complaints from businesses including the silk weavers of France led to violent riots with considerable bloodshed between 1831 and 1834. The export and delivery of cloth became hampered by such violence and orders were lost due to the unsettling situation. In 1844 the *Grande Fabrique* noted that 50,000 looms wove plain and figured cloth while in 1801 this figure was 65,000 (Dumonthier, E. (1909b), p. 21). The break-up of the French Empire meant that the French silk industry, which had previously been able to provide places such as Italy, Switzerland or Germany with cheaper goods, was now subjected to import tariffs and

Cat. 15

Cat. 17

Cat.10

one consequence was the increased cost of French silks. The only light at the end of the tunnel was the change in British law in 1826, which had removed the ban on the import of French fabrics. While damaging to the British textile industry, this ensured that the French with their more efficient looms and reliable dyes regained a new market, spurred on by the Prince Regent, who built the Brighton Pavilion and filled it with both British and French silk fabrics.

Historicism

By the mid-nineteenth century Europe had seen a growing extension of its Empires, through the direct result of exploration, extending trade and missionary routes. Britain was the principal European power that continued to expand and held many countries in its power; acquiring Hong Kong in 1842, Natal in 1843 and Lower Burma in 1852, and claiming sovereignty over New Zealand in 1840 having previously acquired Australia in 1829. Political and social reforms on the continent saw France having known two dynasties, that of the Houses of Bonaparte and Bourbon, and taking Republicanism to its heart. Spain had seen three monarchs and both Italy and Germany had united their separate principalities into national coalitions. France, the Netherlands and Spain had lost much of their colonial power to the British, but still wars were fought for imperial ambitions. In 1867 Russia sold Alaska to the United States, while the French, determined to replace their empire lost in 1815, conquered Algeria in 1834 and expanded its colony in Senegal in the 1850s. Technology advanced and the industrialisation of the late eighteenth and nineteenth centuries opened up areas of the world from Turkey and Egypt to Persia and China, ensuring a quicker means of receiving supplies into Europe as well as providing an export trade to the textile and finance businesses of Europe. Textile production flourished under these conditions, and their styles reflected the diversity of cultures now increasingly interlinked.

Paris by the mid-nineteenth century was one of the world's largest textile manufacturing cities with its income doubling compared with Britain's earnings. Lyon's output of hand loom weaving also saw a healthy increase; in 1852, there were 65,000 looms working and by 1865 this had nearly doubled to 116,000 hand looms, which wove mainly patterned silks (Schober, J. (1930), p. 245). The reigns of both the British Queen Victoria (1819-1901) and Louis Philippe (1774-1850) of France saw a resurgence of textile design styles from the thirteenth and fourteenth centuries to the end of the eighteenth cen-

Cat. 36

Cat. 42

tury. Louis Philippe undertook to refurbish all his palaces with their original designs, and the result was a blend of styles mixing Empire, Neo-Classical and Rococo elements. In Britain, Prince Albert (consort to Queen Victoria) initiated an exhibition which was to display work and industrial craft from around the world, highlighting the extent of the British Empire. Taking place in 1851, The Great Exhibition became the shop window for the many industries. For the textile manufacturer it provided a chance to display magnificent silks, which used new technological advances in yarns and dyes. Designs were bold, large-scale and the craftsmanship of the weaver abounded; fabrics on display included brocatelles, velvets, satins and grand brocades.

Two significant events during the mid-nineteenth century helped to shape the design styles of this period. In 1834 the Palace of Westminster – Britain's Parliament – was gutted by a fire; Augustus Welby Northmore Pugin, along with Charles Barry, was commissioned to re-build Britain's seat of governmental power. Work began in the 1830s, and finished in 1852 with the state opening of Parliament, when both the House of Lords and Commons were finished. Pugin based his interior design work on a distinctive Gothic look; furniture, wallpaper and textiles were decorated with Medieval and Renaissance elements. Paris, meanwhile, had suffered tremendous losses to its historical buildings through the bloody revolutions and uprisings it had endured. It was decided in 1853 that Paris should be rebuilt under the jurisdiction of Baron George Eugène Haussmann. Over the next eighteen years Paris was re-developed from a Medieval city with rambling streets into one containing new boulevards, roads, parks and buildings. Key prominent places were restored, such as the cathedral of Notre Dame and the reliquary shrine of Sainte Chapelle; new buildings were built based on a romantic ideal of Medieval architecture and decorative arts. The re-emergence of design styles did not necessarily come from architecture, but also from literature; in Britain and France the Elizabethan and Troubadour looks were inspired by novels which illustrated the period with chivalry and romance. Consumers wanted to surround themselves with items which helped to convey these written-about high ideals.

In France Eugène Viollet-le-Duc produced architectural and detailed drawings of decorative objects from Gothic sources. In keeping with this fashion, Lemire père et fils produced for the *Paris Exposition Universelle* in 1855 a luxurious brocaded silk satin using silver and gold in the motif; it took its inspiration from design elements of the seventh and eighth centuries (**cat no 28**). The design was intended to be used for ecclesiastical wear and was made into a chasuble for the exhibition. Other decorative art forms used Gothic inspiration to their benefit; for example the shop Savary had a display made depicting its wares and used as its backdrop a blind which was inspired by Gothic stained glass (**cat no 33**). Such an act could only have come from the work of Viollet-le-Duc and the restorative building work at Sainte Chapelle.

Cat. 28

Cat. 34

Manufacturers such as Tassinari or Prelle produced cloth which incorporated classical Etruscan elements mixed with imagery sourced from other earlier designed fabric. The silk sample (**cat no 53**) shows imagery which was inspired by designs after Dugourc, for the Spanish Royal Court in the late eighteenth century. The imagery was combined with Etruscan patterning, producing a bizarre decorative look; it was woven using the newly discovered aniline dyes, which were a must for any wealthy client. Rococo and Baroque-inspired designs were mixed with other style eras; woven fabrics were now not of one distinct style but of several historical decorative art styles.

A popular fabric during this era was velvet, whether silk ciselé or Utrecht velvet (cloth which is made from a mix of linen and goat or horse hair) (**cat no 45, 46 and 47**). The bourgeois upholstered their furniture in velvets which depicted Classical elements of sirens, mascarons, puttis or huge floral bouquets, mixing styles from the Baroque, Renaissance and Classical eras. These cloths were either upholstered onto chairs or sofas, or they lined walls to shine and show the exuberance of the owner. Often the owners of these commissioned cloths were as 'exotic' and flamboyant as the silks they purchased. La Païva, a courtesan of the mid-nineteenth century, built herself a great house on the Champs-Elysées, which later became known as the Hôtel de Païva. The house featured a Turkish-inspired bathroom with an onyx bathtub. The hallway displayed a grand marble staircase, with the main drawing room being a combination of Renaissance and Baroque styles. The rooms were filled with expensive fixtures and ornaments and the cloths woven by the best Lyonnais silk mills provided lavish silks and velvets befitting the surroundings (**cat no 43 & 44**).

Decorating one's house was not just the preserve of women; men too decorated their homes with opulence. William Williams Hope, one of the wealthiest and eccentric men in the world during the mid-nineteenth century, bought the Hôtel de Monaco in 1838 and set about re-modelling it. He finally moved into his residence in November 1842, and again the place was decorated in a mix of styles featuring Etruscan, Rococo, Baroque and Renaissance. One of the silks chosen for his palace was a silk lampas of the late Baroque era (**cat no 20**). It is not known if this cloth was used for wall coverings or for upholstery, but its brilliant colour of crimson red and gold would have been a stunning feature to any room.

Firms would weave Baroque fabrics alongside Neo-Classical silks, or they took their inspiration from work already being produced for specific projects. The silk merchant Cartier et Fils produced a silk with very slight pattern variations to the fabric that was illustrated by and Decloux and Doury in the publication on Sainte Chapelle. The design was appropriately named *Sainte Chapelle* (**cat no 32**), it was also produced as a printed chintz by the Alsatian print manufacturer Thierry Mieg. It is not fully known but the two firms may have been working on the same project and supplied the same client; in

Cat. 32

Cat. 44

Cat. 53

fact it could have also been supplied to the project at Sainte Chapelle. Such a method of the same pattern being produced by two or even three different manufacturing methods was not uncommon. Grand Frères and its successor, Tassinari et Chatel, also wove magnificent large-scale designs; one depicts pheasants surrounded by scrolling architectural elements in the Baroque style, called *Faisan Doré* (Golden Pheasant) (**cat no 35**), woven in vivid colours and using the aniline dye discovered by Perkins in 1856. Such patterns were woven for the *nouveaux riches*, not just those in Europe but also for increasingly wealthy countries such as America. For example, for Prelle in 1867, a Monsieur Roux designed a silk combining Renaissance and Baroque features called *Van Dyke*; this piece was later re-woven in the 1880s for the American financiers, the Vanderbilts (**cat no 40**). *Faisan Doré* (Golden Pheasant) was also later woven by Tassinari et Chatel and supplied to the American firm F. Schumacher, for the wealthy East Coast clients.

With this bewildering array of different design styles, publications in both America and Europe appeared to help the consumer decorate their homes. In *The Architecture of Country Houses* by A. J. Downing, published in America in 1861, Downing suggested that the Elizabethan style was appropriate for those individuals who had moved from Europe to America. He also suggested that the Neo-Rococo styles were particularly suitable for use on newly improved furniture, including the spring-upholstered sofa. Furniture, which was a few decades earlier criticised, being considered meagre, sparse or downright ugly, was now given new credence. Curtains which were once fussy, ornate or too simple in style were now used to help convey a particular design style for a room. Variety of choice and styles had now become a decorative style of its own.

The emergence of newer more efficient manufacturing methods led to the growth of a new market sector, that of the middle classes; these new rich consumers sought a variety of design choice. Manufacturers were happy to oblige, producing a wealth of patterns, which were manufactured rapidly, being replaced with more patterns once they were sold. Fabrics could often be produced more quickly and in some cases more cheaply; mass production was the new way. The traditional approach of commissioning textiles from a mill was still viable for only the rich sector of the market.

The *Grande Fabrique* continued in its traditional organisation; however, silk merchants provided a design service to their clients. A silk merchant would show his customer a range of designs and fabric types which he had to offer. These fabrics were in turn provided either via independent weavers who worked within a radius of a few miles, or by the company's own looms. Customers were never aware of how products were made; their preoccupation was their décor and what design and colour combinations they had to choose. They would visit the silk merchants in Paris or London – very rarely did they visit the factory and they would certainly not see the conditions the weavers had to work in. In each merchant's premises a sumptuous display of luxurious

Cat. 20　　　Cat. 40

Cat. 35

cloth was set up to show the customer a sample of fabrics, named appro samples. An order would be placed for the fabric seen and the specific requirements of the individual customer were woven.

As designs literally inspired by history reached their peak of fashion in this period, contemporary critics decided that what was needed was a new approach to design, one that allowed new ideas to circulate. What is today the Victoria & Albert Museum was set up in London to store and display some of the items that had been exhibited at the 1851 Great Exhibition. The Art and Industry Museum of Lyon, founded in 1864 by the Chamber of Commerce, commenced this idea in France too. Both institutions provided manufacturers with inspiration as well as educating the public about well-designed products, many from other cultures. Equally influential were publications containing colour plates which revealed for the first time ornament from other cultures, in particular Islamic and Persian decoration.

Two Frenchmen, Joseph Pierre Girault de Pragney and Pascal-Xavier Coste, were the first to produce publications in 1832 and 1839, respectively, which detailed elevations and drawings of the famous Alhambra. In 1842 Owen Jones produced the comprehensive two-volume publication on the Alhambra. All these publications became influential books for design inspiration. *The Grammar of Ornament* followed in 1856 and was to become the bible for design ideas to this day. It displayed detailed drawings from architectural sources around the world. The publication featured ornate colour lithograph plates that allowed the manufacturer to directly copy the designs (which Jones opposed) or to use his theories to form new patterns. Well into the 1880s, his concepts influenced weavers such as Warner & Ramm, Daniel Keith & Co, Daniel Walters and Shoesmith of London and, in Lyon, Mathevon et Bouvard, Lemire, Prelle, Lamy and Grand Frères; all sought inspiration from these publications, examples of which can be seen in this catalogue (**cat no 21, 22 and 23**). A consequence of the publication is that variations of the same design could be woven by several European manufacturers. The success of *The Grammar of Ornament* inspired further publications such as *La Décoration Arabe* by Prisse d'Avennes. Published in 1885, it depicts detailed aspects of centuries of Islamic decoration. Silk manufacturers not only reproduced the fabric designs depicted but also incorporated architectural design elements from fritware and architectural tiles to mosaics and decorative objects. Examples of such interpretations include the silk *Byzantine* (**cat no 25**), which was inspired by architectural tiling seen in *The Grammar of Ornament*. The inception of the Art Workers Guild in 1884 saw architects, designers, artists and manufacturers further the philosophy of a cross-disciplinary approach and a new approach to design and the making process started to emerge.

Cat. 23

Cat. 21

Cat. 22

Aesthetic and Arts & Crafts

In the later nineteenth century International Exhibitions held in both Philadelphia (1876) and Paris (1878) saw an increase of textile production in the Japanese style; this style became known as the Aesthetic. A designer predominant during this era was Christopher Dresser, who produced industrial designs for ceramic tiles made by Minton, textile designs for Warner & Sons and J. W. & C. Ward of Halifax, and wallpaper for John Perry and Desfossé et Karth, to name but a few. His images were elegant, stylised and simple, influenced by Japanese wares and decorative work of either cloisonné or lacquer effects (**cat no 57**). This Aesthetic style provided a new inspiration for manufacturers, who increasingly began to commission designs from a younger generation of designers who served many industries. These unique designs were intended to be used for mass production and affordable to most sectors of the populace and not just the elite. Designers such as Dresser considered the manufacture of their designs, so that they were affordable to many. Dresser promoted the use of brown and blue paper (this paper was used to wrap sugar and groceries in and was cheap to manufacture) as being ideal to make wallpaper with. It was hoped that designing for all sectors of the market would prevent the copying of designs by several manufacturers, which had been seen previously with the glut of publications during the mid-nineteenth century.

The mass production of similar types of patterns caused a reaction by the elite public, which now started to herald the craft-based industries rather than the mechanised industries. Nevertheless, even in hand-powered weaving 'factories', weavers worked a six-day week, from 6am until 9pm in summer with the time being restricted to 7am until 7pm in winter. Each weaver would be a specialist in a certain type of fabric structure and would weave between five and ten particular designs only. Weaving times varied with the complexity of cloth. In some cases a hand-loom weaver could weave between one and two inches a day, but for easier damask designs this could increase to fifteen yards per day. Conditions could be hard and cramped with noise levels being extreme. The weaver owned his tools, with the mill owning the loom and the silk yarn. Silk was a precious commodity and any loss had to be paid for. The yarn was weighed prior to weaving and then the cloth weighed at the end; any discrepancy in weight was charged to the weaver as wastage and so the weaver had to be skilled not only in craft but also in the use of the yarn. As a result, weavers were justifiably proud of their work – producing cloths such as *Hatton* (**cat no 59**) designed by Bruce Talbert and woven by the master weaver, Burrows, on 18 May 1877 for Warner & Ramm. This was to be the last era of great prosperity for hand-weavers.

The Arts & Crafts movement was established with the formation of the Arts & Crafts Exhibition Society in 1887; its intention was to bring to the public well-made goods pro-

Cat. 25

Cat. 57

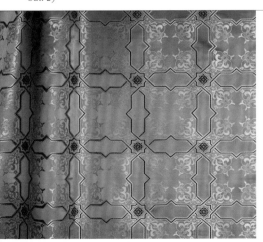

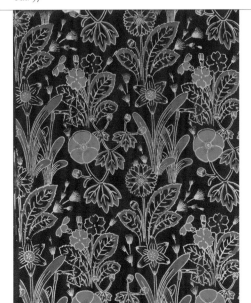

duced by craftsmen at the helm of their craft. Prior to this event, those involved within the movement – such as William Morris, Edward Burne Jones and Dante Gabriel Rossetti – had already attempted to bridge the void between designer, craftsman and industry. They gave birth to the Arts & Crafts style, during the 1850s and 1860s, as a result of a dislike of industrial goods, which were mass produced cheaply, in large quantities and were often of a poor standard. By 1860 the British textile industry had suffered greatly as a consequence of the lifting of the duty on imported foreign silks; what was beneficial to France proved catastrophic to Britain. In the first year of the lifting of the duty, imports into Britain almost doubled. The Lyonnais weavers were able to produce hand-woven silks at a lower cost, and they had the bonus at this time of Paris dictating trends for both fashion and furnishing fabrics. As the British suffered, some manufacturers went out of business or were amalgamated with other firms because they could not compete with such fierce competition, and an economic downturn began. Thus the ideals for the movement were based on the concept that creative works of art and a robust society were interlinked.

As a style, the Arts & Crafts and Art Nouveau movements sat easily alongside other decorative styles such as the Aesthetic, which embraced all things Japanese. The popularity for Japanese goods inspired the decorative arts from the early 1870s and provided a new design direction for the British textile industry, enabling manufacturers to produce cloth which was different in style to any other previously known. Designs were provided by industrial designers and architects, all home grown. Owen Jones, having produced several publications that inspired designers to look at the architecture, textiles and decorative wares of different cultures for inspiration, provided his own unique designs to the British textile trade. (There is no extant primary evidence which shows that Jones supplied unique designs to the French textile industry.) Other designers such as B. J. Talbert, E. W. Godwin and Christopher Dresser all provided stylish designs, which were far less rigid in interpretation than those characteristic of the previous historicist style. Like Dresser, Talbert worked in the Aesthetic manner, producing free-flowing designs of floral branches with insects, birds and animals. The fabric illustrated within this catalogue was produced in 1877 both in wool and as a silk damask. The silk was woven by Warner & Ramm, while the wool was produced by J. W. & C. Ward of Halifax, quite possibly for the same client. Both these mills were among Britain's best producers of silk and wool, respectively (**cat no 58**).

The growing interest in Far Eastern design and ornamentation led to the establishment of specialist shops that carried imported stock; Liberty & Co of Regent Street opened in 1875 and sold Japanese and Asian goods. In the same year William Morris established what was to become the firm Morris & Company. He wanted this new company to carry forward his mission to 'Have nothing in your houses that you know not

Cat. 59

to be useful, or believe to be beautiful' (William Morris, 1882). He shunned industrial processes, which were now a large part of the textile industry, and was horrified by the conditions the mill workers had to work in. He undertook to use traditional craftsmen for his goods. Hating the new artificial dyes, which had emerged since the mid-nineteenth century, he experimented with natural dyestuffs – in particular madder, weld and indigo – perfecting his ability to provide a stable colour that could dye yarn as well as be applied to cloth by block or roller printing. He worked with craft-based factories to perfect the techniques of production, from the initial stages of producing blocks to the process of printing itself. Working closely with the craftsmen, he realised that by allowing the printer to control and work with the design, the cloth would often be improved at its finish. He was certainly not shy of working with large firms, having worked with the block printer, Thomas Clarkson of Carlisle, which produced a series of block prints that Morris & Co stocked. He worked particularly closely with the firm Thomas Wardle, which helped him refine his dying techniques. Wardle's were known as manufacturers of printing cloth, for many different applications such as canvas cloths to be used in kits for amateur embroiderers or block printing old patterns for established firms such as Watt & Co, and depicted by *Royal Burgundy* (**cat no 62**).

Morris also worked on specific projects with selected and specialist manufacturers, such as a large project intended for the royal palace, St James, for which Morris contracted out the silk, *St James*, to Warner & Ramm in order that the weaving could be supplied in time. For textile manufacturers meeting a deadline was crucial; any delays in production would cost the mill dearly in further orders, particularly if the project was for a royal client. Morris had to bear this in mind, for his chosen method of production was often slow and labour-intensive, whereas the then-current industrial methods were already much quicker and not so labour-intensive. Morris used such constraints of the specialist craft production to his benefit, marketing his items carefully as being of the highest quality and skilfully produced. Excited by the texture and tactile quality of the cloth, he used natural fibres and produced many different cloth types, from damasks, brocades and velvets in a mixture of substrates, to embroideries, tapestries, challis, carpets (both machine and hand knotted), as well as printed cottons. All the fabrics at one time or another were made at Merton Abbey, his factory based on the outskirts of London. To produce such an array of products, which also included wallpapers, was unusual; mills more typically provided goods of only one or two types. The variety of Morris products is well represented here. Issued by Morris & Co between 1875 and 1940, from 1940 onwards the designs were subsequently split between Arthur Sanderson & Sons for wallpaper and, for fabrics, Warner & Sons, Liberty & Co, and Stead McAlpin, which had taken over the patterns of Thomas Clarkson. The designs vary from rare pieces such as *Brer Rabbit* (**cat no 60: 8**) to well-known pieces such as *Strawberry Thief*

Cat. 58   Cat. 62

(**cat no 60: 15**) or *Medway* (**cat no 60: 14**); the early pieces were made using natural dyes and traditional methods of resist block printing using indigo and madder dyes. The later piece, *Windrush*, was printed by Stead McAlpin and sold through the Old Bleach Linen Co. It clearly shows the move from craft to an industrial process, using aniline rather than natural dyes, and is a distinctive move away from Morris's design thinking.

A lesser-known firm influenced by the Arts & Crafts ethos was St Edmundsbury Weaving Works, founded by Edmund Hunter in 1901. Hunter had previously been a designer at the established Silver Studio. St Edmundsbury Weaving Works was based in Haslemere, a place which had a collective group of artist-craftsmen named the Haslemere Peasant Industries. This community was set up in 1894, and had various workshops creating pottery, woodwork, bookbinding, fresco painting, plaster work and textiles. Hunter's first venture into his own business provided ecclesiastical fabrics, employing simplified iconographic motifs, which were ideal for ecclesiastical use. Like Morris they provided a craft-based service, with cloth being produced by the traditional hand-craft methods. Hunter produced as a tapestry weave a fabric called *Vineyard* (**cat no 65**) woven in 1903; it shows a marked similarity to the design *Vine* produced by Dearle for Morris & Co in 1890. The firm also had close links with the silk weaving operation owned by Luther Hooper, which too was based in Haslemere. He wove an array of products consisting of a mix of silk, worsted and cotton cloths. It is Hooper who can be credited for teaching Hunter the technical aspects of weaving, a brilliant technician of weaving who sadly lacked the business acumen of William Morris and was thus never able to make a great name for himself.

St Edmundsbury Weaving Works was able to marry good design and craft in its products. Its design was based around Edmund Hunter's interest in then-radical sources of design inspiration, such as theosophy and astrology. In 1908 the firm moved to larger premises in Letchworth Garden City. This was so that they could install power looms as well as the hand looms that moved with them. The move allowed them to broaden their range to include domestic furnishing fabrics such as *The Path* (**cat no 67a**), designed by Hunter in 1904. From 1916 this cloth was produced as both a furnishing and apparel fabric; the clothes fabric was sold to Saville Row tailors, in particular Dunhill, and was intended to line coats or be made into scarves (**cat no 67b**).

John Illingworth Kay, another designer who also trained at the Silver Studio, provided designs to many European firms; he was greatly influenced by the Aesthetic movement and had a deep love of oriental gardens, which the piece illustrated in the catalogue is clearly influenced by (**cat no 61**). Designed in 1893, it was intended to be a wallpaper, but it was sold to the furnishing print manufacturer Richard Stanway who produced the design as a roller-printed velveteen in 1895. What this continues to show is that the same design could be adapted or reproduced directly by other manufacturing methods. Charles

Cat. 60: 8

Cat. 60: 14

Cat. 60: 15

Fredrick Annesley Voysey, a well-regarded architect and designer, supplied many firms with designs including A. H. Lee, Turnbull & Stockdale, G. P. & J. Baker, to name but a few. In 1893, for Baker's he provided the watercolour design depicting birds and scrolling acanthus leaves, which they produced as a printed velveteen for their client base; a sample of *Bird* is illustrated here (**cat no 63**).

The Arts & Crafts movement's philosophy and teachings spread to other countries, becoming popular in America from 1890 onwards. This was due in part to the resulting growth of the economy during the nineteenth century, seeing rapid industrial expansion and urbanisation. It was the Arts & Crafts movement which provided an alternative to the harsh urbanised lifestyle; individual designer-makers set up studios alongside craft-based villages. Homes became a mix of American Indian and Mexican folk art with Arts & Crafts individually made pieces. The Society of Blue and White Needlework, based in Deerfield, Massachusetts, followed the principles and teachings of Morris & Co, concentrating on a limited colour scheme using indigo blue as the predominant colour for their work. The Arts & Crafts movement has made a powerful and persuasive contribution to the decorative art styles. Its influence runs through Modernism, the Omega Workshop and the Bauhaus, up to present-day contemporary craft practices, with many current designer-makers having established their roots in the principles of the Arts & Crafts teachings.

Cat. 67a

Cat. 61

Cat. 63

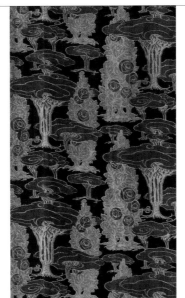

French, Lyon, probably designed by Joseph Bourne
and manufactured by Reboul et Fontebrune, c1785
a) 212 × 55 cm (83 ½ × 21 ¾ in), not illustrated
b) 213 × 55 cm (84 × 21 ¾ in)
Silk liseré

A silk lampas in ice blue with a large pattern
repeat (approximately 255–260 cm in length)
in cream and beige originally consisting of four
registers and produced in the last years of the
Ancien Régime between 1785 and 1793. The two
pieces together form one repeat depicting a
platform on which stand two priestesses from
Antiquity, pouring oil or perfume onto sacrificial
flames on a dias; the second register shows
two deer standing addorsed, eating leaves from
branches that grow from a platform on which they
stand; the third register depicts two Enceladus
Gods holding up a table on which rests an urn.
Another register, of a Caryatid looking down onto a
plaque, depicts an avenue of trees, held in place by
two Griffins. The registers are linked by branches,
leaves, garlands and ribbons.

We have attributed the design to Joseph
Bourne, who worked in Lyon in the late eighteenth
century. His textiles illustrate figures and animals
in a style identical to ours (Tassinari, B. (2005),
p. 151). His inspiration would have come from
the ancient objects that were excavated in 1709
when Herculaneum was discovered and later, the
excavations at Pompeii in 1748. These excavations
provided the impetus for the Neo-Classical style. A
very similar design to our silk was woven between
1785 and 1788 and used in the small bedroom of the
Comtesse d'Artois at Compiègne.

The manufacturer was probably the Lyon firm
Reboul et Fontebrune, who wove variations of
these designs on a draw-loom. We compared our
silk with similar examples by this manufacturer at
the Musée des Tissus in Lyon and found the same
weaving flaws in the exact same places. Also, the
sett (the weaving structure) was identical in both
cases. For these technical as well as for stylistic
reasons, we have attributed our silk to Reboul et
Fontebrune.

Small firms and 'cottage' silk weavers would
produce only a small number of designs in one
particular manufacturing method such as the
lampas technique for which Reboul et Fontebrune
were renowned. They varied their design repertoire
by slightly altering the design of some of the
motifs. Consequently, silks of similar designs can
be found in several collections. There are three
lengths of a very similar silk in the Abegg-Stiftung
in Bern (inv. 1754) and other silks of a stylistically
similar design are in the Musée des Tissus in Lyon
(DET 131, 136 and 154). An identical example of our
textile, but with its full repeat, is in the Musée des
Tissus in Lyon (DET 158).

2 | *Royal French Curtains Embroidered in the Fête Champêtre Style*

French, commissioned by the Duc de Penthièvre
for l'Hôtel de Toulouse in Paris, c1787
365 × 209 cm (144 × 82 in) each curtain
Embroidered silk chain stitch on satin ground

A very rare and spectacular pair of curtains, which
are virtually in perfect condition. The curtains are
French, and were probably made in Lyon, and are
attributed to the designer Philippe de la Salle. They
were commissioned by Louis-Jean Marie de Bourbon,
Duc de Penthièvre (1725-93), c1787, for the chambre
à balustre at the Hôtel de Toulouse in Paris.

The curtains are each bordered on three
sides with contemporary passementerie, and are
comprised of three loom widths of silk satin. The
centre is decorated in the Marie Antoinette Fête
Champêtre style, consisting of floral garlands,
which link the central vertical motifs of a bird
feeding its young, a tambourine and panpipes and a
basket overflowing with fruit, flowers and bagpipes
with a shepherdess's hat draped alongside. The
motifs are linked by a blue or pink trailing ribbon.

France was renowned for its silk weaving and
textile production during the eighteenth century,
due in no small part to royal patronage. There
are abundant examples of silks woven to royal
commission but embroideries were far more time
consuming, and as a consequence, they are much
rarer than brocaded silk. Other embroideries
from this suite are in the Mobilier National, no.
GMMP 863, the Cleveland Museum of Art (the bed
is attributed to Georges Jacob and is ex-Richard
Wallace collection) and the Metropolitan Museum
of Art (ex-Kress collection, ex-Duveen chairs and
embroidered hangings). Some of these pieces
have been illustrated in Arizzoli-Clémentel, P. and
Coural, J. (1988), p. 124, and Verlet, P. (1963), pp.
304-05. An embroidered hanging, brought into the
Garde-Meuble in the nineteenth century by Louis
Philippe when Duc d'Orléans, was exhibited in
*Soieries de Lyon: Commandes Royales Au XVIII (1730-
1800)*, held at the Musée des Tissus in Lyon, which
ran from December 1988 to March 1989, no. 56.
The Duc de Penthièvre (1725-1793) was the son
of the Comte de Toulouse and the last survivor of
the legitimised descendants of Louis XIV. He was
fabulously rich. His daughter-in-law, the Princesse
de Lamballe, was a friend and confidente to Marie
Antionette, thus ensuring a strong link to the Royal
Court. The duke's daughter, Louise-Marie-Adelaide,
Duchesse d'Orléans, was the mother of the future
King Louis Philippe of France who reigned from
1830 to 1848.

34

3 | *Etruscan-style Silk*

French, Lyon, probably a royal commission,
in the style of Jean-Démosthène Dugourc
manufactured by Camille Pernon, c1795
213 × 54.5 cm (83 ½ × 21 ½ in)
Silk strié liseré

A magnificent silk woven in a strié ice blue
with the design depicted in white. The length
of the repeat, which is large in scale, depicts a
rectangular medallion of cavaliers on horseback
trotting through woodland. The medallion is
guarded by two sphinxes. There is a fern spray
with Nemean the lion; on either side of Nemean
are two angry geese. At the base of this fern
display is a plaque with two putti and dancing
above are a pair of addorsed satyrs. The central
section of the panel features the god Pan with
an elaborate floral display balanced upon his
head. Around the edge of these main motifs are
floral trails surrounded by insects and birds
and the Greek mythological figure Arachne,
half woman and half butterfly. It is said she
was a fine weaver but, unfortunately, she had a
contest with Athena the Goddess of weaving to
prove her supremacy in the art of weaving. She
angered Athena and was shamed and as a result
she hung herself.

The putti and the satyrs also feature in a
spectacular yellow, brown, white and black silk
lampas designed by Jean-Démosthène Dugourc
for Charles IV of Spain, for the ballroom of the
Casita del Labrador at Aranjuez, woven by
Pernon in 1797, published in Arizzoli-Clémentel,
P. and Coural, J. (1988), p. 130; Gruber, A. (ed.)
(1994), p. 124; and Flemming, E. (1928), p. 115. A
silk from the same commission is in the Musée
des Tissus in Lyon (inv. no. 24.804/2) as well as
in the Victoria & Albert Museum in London. The
Lyon piece was also exhibited at the Musée des
Tissus, no. 80, in the exhibition *Soieries de Lyon
Commandes Royales au XVIII Siècle (1730-1800)*,
which ran from December 1988 to March 1989.

It is not known who our cloth was woven for,
but it is assumed that Camille Pernon was the
weaver due to several design elements which
appear in other Pernon silks. Also, there are
some general similarities with the Directoire
period (1795-99) silks, particularly in the way
the different design elements are grouped in
blocks.

4 | Verdures du Vatican

French, Lyon, designed by Jean-Démosthène Dugourc, originally for King Carlos IV of Spain and manufactured to order by Camille Pernon in 1799
268 × 73.5 cm (105 ½ × 29 in) and 291 × 67cm (114 ¾ × 26 ¼ in)
Silk lampas with applied embroidered silk and chenille panel details

A spectacular pair of Neo-Classical woven wall panels, with applied central, octagonal embroidered vignettes, designed by Jean-Démosthène Dugourc for the Spanish King Carlos IV and woven to order by Camille Pernon. These wall panels were commissioned for the billiard room at the Casita del Labrador in Aranjuez, one of the Spanish royal residences. They are still *in situ* at Aranjuez and a few single panels remain outside of Spain. Both these panels are from the Duchess of Westminster's estate; one panel bears a hand-written label which possibly says the Countess [of] Grosvenor. The pieces bear no fading, wear and very few tack marks from being stretched and fixed to a wall. Thus it has been assumed that the pieces were never used or had very little use.

Each hanging is embroidered in the centre with fine vignettes of views. The top and bottom of the textiles also have smaller embroidered sections of different-sized vignettes with birds, running lions, urns of flowers, butterflies, salamanders, snails and lizards, and birds in their nests. All these scenes are framed by garlands of poppies. Other, single, panels from this commission depicting Dugourc's *The Pheasants* are in the Boston Museum of Fine Arts, the Art Institute of Chicago, the Metropolitan Museum of Art and the Rhode Island School of Design. To our knowledge, only the Abegg-Stiftung in Bern has one scenic panel (inv. no. 4925) similar to this pair, which is illustrated in the publication by Jolly, A. (2005), pp. 178-81, alongside a pair of panels depicting *The Pheasants*. Other publications – Junquera, J. J. (1979), pp. 132-33; Hartmann, S. (1980), p. 212; Arizzoli-Clémentel, P. and Coural, J. (1988) p. 136; and the Musée des Arts Décoratif exhibition catalogue Anon (1984), p. 91 – also feature the design for this silk ensemble. The pieces are also illustrated in Schoeser, M. (2007), p. 90.

The original watercolour design by Dugourc, held in the Musée des Tissus in Lyon, shows two scenic wall panels similar to these hung either side of a central panel with cock, vase of flowers and confronting pheasants, entitled *The Pheasants*. The four panels are framed by a dark-coloured floral border. This design was exhibited in the exhibition *Soieries de Lyon: Commandes Royales au XVIIIe Siècle (1730-1800)* held at the Musée des Tissus in Lyon, no. 106, from December 1988 to March 1989. Both the silk pieces are now held at the Metropolitan Museum of Art in New York.

Jean-Démosthène Dugourc was trained as an architect and spent time in Italy where he became familiar with the antique motifs that Raphael had revived in his fresco decorations for the Loggia at the Vatican. Dugourc entitled this particular group of silks *Verdures du Vatican* after the frescos that he had seen at the Vatican in Rome.

5 | *En Candélabre (Ornate Column)*
French, Lyon, by Bissardon, Cousin et Bony,
painted velvet vases and rhyta probably by
Vauchelet, c1795–1810
330 × 55 cm (189 × 21 ½ in) each panel
Silk chenille embroidery and appliqué painted silk
velvet upon a gros de Tours silk ground

A magnificent pair of embroidered wall panels in
the Etruscan style. Each panel depicts two rhyta,
which rest on a thin, sceptre-like plinth and are
separated from each other by a floral urn. Each
rhyton is shaped like a vase with the head of a wild
animal hunted for sport. Upon one panel is a wolf
and a boar and on the other a boar and a stag. The
rhyta are painted to emulate a copper patina and
are painted with classical sirens and overflow with
fruit and foliage. The floral urns, with bouquets of
roses, other flowers and wisps of foliage, hang from
scrolling *rinceaux* and palmettes.

Each panel is embroidered by hand in silk
chenille in a satin and flat stitch on a gros de Tours
ground. The hand-painted silk velvet urns and
rhyta were probably made by the Lyonnais firm
Vauchelet, renowned specialists for such work. The
vase and rhyton are both appliquéd onto the silk
satin ground cloth in a corded stitch. The panels
were obviously intended as wall hangings, because
of their long length and design repeat.

An identical embroidered panel to ours, in
pristine condition, is in the Musée des Tissus in
Lyon (DET 2832), which the museum dates to the
Directoire period (1795–99). The embroidery is
illustrated in Riley, N. (2003), p. 207; Sano, T. (1976),
pl. 17; and Calavas, A. (1905), pl. XV, who dated it to
the Empire period (1800–14).

We have not yet identified the specific
commission nor the exact date of manufacture.
However, the design is extremely refined and the
quality of manufacture high, which would indicate
an aristocratic or wealthy private commission. The
restrained style of decoration brings to mind the
Etruscan revival interiors of the Directoire period
(1795–99) at the Hôtel de Bourienne in Paris. More
elaborate embroidered hangings were made for
Napoleon for Versailles, Saint Cloud, Compiègne
and Fontainebleau, all decorated with the familiar
Imperial emblems of laurel leaves, Greek, Egyptian
and Roman ornament with animals and bees
scattered among the connecting *rinceaux*. These
commissions were almost certainly the exclusive
preserve of the Lyonnais firm Bissardon, Cousin
et Bony, which, under the designer-manufacturer
Jean-François Bony, produced some breathtaking
designs for both dress and interior settings. These
included the bedroom of Queen Marie Antionette
in 1787, the mantles to the 1804 coronation robes of
both Napoleon and Josephine and an elaborate silk
embroidered wall hanging featuring painted velvet
and chenille embroidery for the palace of Versailles
in 1811.

6 | *Border of Laurel Leaves*

French, Lyon, manufactured by Camille Pernon, for Napoleon Bonaparte's Library at the Palace of Saint Cloud, 1804–07

208 × 48 cm (82 × 19 in)

Satin brocaded with metal thread

A border of brocaded metal thread on a red 'corn poppy' silk satin ground. The commission for this border textile and its companion wall hanging was tendered to Camille Pernon in 1802 for the library of the First Consul, Napoleon Bonaparte, at the Palace of Saint Cloud. The fabric was woven in a 'corn poppy' (ponceau) and gold colourway by the manufacturer Camille Pernon in 1804–05. The design depicts acanthus leaf scrolls and a palmette of laurel leaves. The wide and imposing border would have surrounded a green satin damask with large palm leaves, which would have covered the walls of the library. More of this fabric was woven and delivered in 1807. The green silk damask with palm design and pink/red silk laurel leaf border also decorated the Salon or Grand Study (Grand Cabinet) of the Emperor at Saint Cloud and remained *in situ* until April 1813.

These hangings, with their borders, became notorious because the dyes were fugitive and faded within little more than a year, thus attracting the Emperor's ire. The resulting correspondence with the Lyon Chamber of Commerce is indicative of his obsessive and perfectionist personality. Napoleon pointed out to his ministers that visiting foreign dignitaries would gain a very bad impression of the State of France and a very bad impression of the silk mills in Lyon (a note from Napoleon to his Minister of the Interior Cretet 1807: '…*la tenture verte avec les bordures roses tissues en or, qui a été placée dans le Cabinet de Sa Majesté à Saint-Cloud il n'y a pas beaucoup plus d'un an est déjà passée … Les syndics se transporteront chez le fabricant, examineront d'où provient le vice de fabrication et rendront un compte qui sera mis sous les yeux de Sa Majesté. Les étrangers qui voient dans un tel état des ameulements aussi modernes ne peuvent que prendre une très mauvaise idée de la fabrique de Lyon.'* Coural, J. (1980), p. 307).

As a result, all the textiles Camille Pernon supplied to the *Garde-Meuble* were checked for dye fastness and only those dyed with yellow and crimson were considered acceptable: '…*que de toutes les étoffes livrées par M.Pernon les beaux jaunes et les cramoisis sont les seuls qui aient été trouvés solides et susceptible de durer longtemps…'* Coural, J. (1980), p. 308.

Of the FF 85,786 owed to Camille Pernon, FF 42,909 were withheld in lieu of damages with instructions from the Emperor to keep this money in Lyon for research into perfecting dyes. Pernon, already an old man, was dead by 1808.

In addition to Saint Cloud, the combination of green damask with large palm leaf design and red/pink 'corn poppy' and gold border with laurel leaf design was also used at the Laeken Palace in 1805 (Emperor's Office), the Tuileries Palace in 1809 (anteroom of the Emperor's Private Apartment) and Rohan Palace in Strasbourg in 1809 (Emperor's Audience Hall). Subsequent weavings of this design were commissioned in lapis blue for the bedchamber of the petit appartement of the Empress Josephine at the palace of Fontainebleau in 1809. The furnishings were installed in September 1809, just in time for when the court stayed in late September. The border framed hangings and curtains of brocaded rosettes on a white satin ground; the sculptured and gilded chairs by Jacob Desmalter were covered with the same lapis blue satin.

We believe that the border shown here was part of the original commission for Saint Cloud, which was taken down in 1813. Our piece is stamped with the manufacturer number 73508.

This fabric is featured in several publications

including Coural, J. (1980), p. 306; Coural, C. (2002a),
p. 55; Martin, R. (1983), p. 55, Verzier, P. (2002), p.
37. A fragment from the Mobilier National (MM
40.473149) was exhibited in *Soies Tissées, Soies
Brodées Chez L'impératrice Joséphine*, at Malmaison
et Bois-Perau, October 2002 to February 2003, no.
29. Another piece is also held in the collection of
the Mobilier National in Paris, no. GMMP 246/1 (4
m 80 cm).

7 | ***Rosettes***

French, Lyon, probably manufactured by Grand
Frères, 1800-25
64 × 55 cm (25 × 21 ½ in)
Brocaded metal upon a silk cannetillé or armure
ground

A green silk brocaded with small, gold scrollwork
medallions powdered across the cloth. This type
of fabric was often used as lining for ornate
curtain drapes or bed hangings. Similar cloths are
illustrated in Oglesby, C. (1951), p. 180.

A design similar to our silk was woven by Grand
Frères for the interior furnishings of Fontainebleau.
It is not known if our silk was also commissioned
by Napoleon Bonaparte or his successor, Louis
XVIII, or by a wealthy private client.

Grand Frères came to prominence in the year
1808, when the firm took over the weaving order
book of the firm Camille Pernon. They, like Pernon,
continued to weave exquisite fabrics of the highest
quality supplying the wealthy classes and the
French court with their breathtaking fabrics. Grand
Frères was taken over by Tassinari et Chatel in
1871.

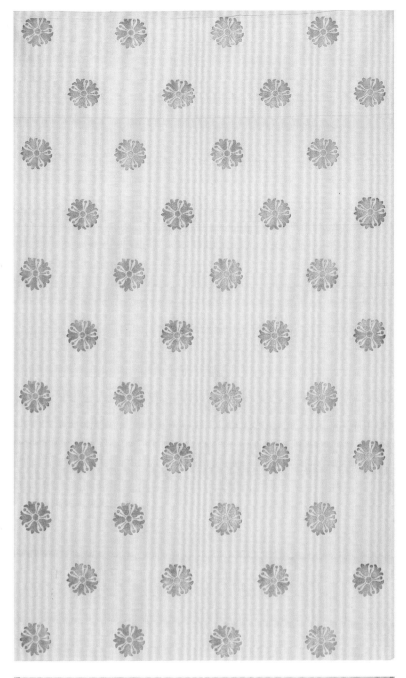

8 **_Marguerites, Star Shape and Stylised Flower_**

French, Lyon, manufactured probably by Bissardon, Cousin et Bony or Grand Frères, c1808–25

a) 60.5 × 55.5 cm (24 × 22 in) in gold on white
b) 50.5 × 55 cm (20 × 21 ½ in) in gold on green
c) 91 × 55.5 cm (36 × 22 in) in gold on white
Brocaded metal and silk taffeta

A half-drop repeat of marguerites woven in gold thread into a taffeta ground, with a similar design showing a four-petalled stylised flower and a star shape on green taffeta.

Designs featuring such simple motifs were popular as linings or under mantels for curtain drapes. A similar design to the _marguerites_ piece, now in the Mobilier National (GMMP1859), was woven c1811 for a bedroom in the _Palais de Compiègne_ (Oglesby, C. (1951), p. 180 and Coural, J. (1980), p. 419). The stylised flower also shows a similarity to a damask supplied to Fontainebleau, for one of the apartments of the Gros Pavillon (Coural, J. (1980), p. 218). We have attributed our silks to Grand Frères or Bissardon, Cousin et Bony, because of their similarity to silks supplied to the Imperial household of Napoleon Bonaparte which feature throughout (Coural, J. (1980), pp. 38–463). Jean-François Bony was born in 1754 and trained in Fine Arts at the École de Beaux-Arts in Lyon, where some years later he returned as a professor until 1810. Upon graduation he became a journeyman, moving to Paris for a year. He returned to Lyon where he produced grand designs for silk weaving and embroidery. Bony's work was of the highest standard and he was later asked to design and produce the coronation robes of the Empress Josephine in 1803–04. In 1774 he went into business with another silk weaver, Jean Pierre Bissardon, and by 1791 they had acquired the famous Ancien Regime firm, Desfarges, which had woven silks for Marie Antoinette for both Versailles and Saint Cloud. In December 1811, the firm became known as Bissardon, Cousin et Bony. They were major suppliers to the Emperor Napoleon for velvets, woven silks and, particularly, embroideries, for Versailles and Fontainebleau. However, these Imperial projects ceased in 1812 for lack of funds as a result of which both Bony and Bissardon retired from manufacturing to concentrate on painting. The weaving firm Chuard took over the business of Bissardon, Cousin et Bony.

9 | Lyre et Coupe (Lyre and Goblet)

French, Lyon, manufactured by Corderier et Lemire, probably made for the Imperial Court, 1800–15
133 × 55.5 cm (52 ½ × 22 ½ in)
Silk lampas

A finely drawn Empire period lampas, woven in ice blue and white silk, depicting a lyre and goblet. Both central motifs are surrounded by a diamond-shaped leaf trail. This style of design was made popular by Napoleon Bonaparte during the Consulate (1799–1804). He decorated his residences with this style of silk depicting Classical motifs, as a result of which fabrics of a similar quality and design began to be produced by many weaving firms such as Davy, Pernon and Lacostat et Cie. Our example relates closely to a silk in the Victoria & Albert Museum (no. T.32-1998), which was woven by Joseph Davy of Lyon in 1813. It has also been documented in the Maison Prelle weaving firm archives no. 273.

The attached label states 'number 4640, (the patron is unknown) Empire lampas 55, blue, grey and cream, Lyre and Goblet'. A smaller, older label refers to the manufacturer Monsieur Lemire with the number 748 (it is believed that this number is for an unknown client).
Corderier et Lemire began weaving at the end of the Revolution in 1799. They were successors to the firm Dechazelle, which had supplied the *Grande Fabrique* with cloth from the mid-eighteenth century until 1792 when the French Revolution affected their trade. In 1811–12 they were granted the rights, along with Chuard, to weave for Versailles and Le Grand Trianon. The firm continued to weave for many prestigious places and clients including the Imperial Russian court of Tsar Alexander II. In 1865 the firm was taken over by Lamy et Giraud, and is today owned by Prelle et Cie.

10 | ***Chair Seat and Back Woven in Crimson and Two-Tone Gold***
French, Lyon, manufactured probably by Grand Frères for Cartier et Fils 1808–15
130 × 56 cm (51 × 22 in)
Brocaded metal silk liseré satin

This elegant furnishing silk shows three elements for an armchair – a back and seat panel with a front seat border motif and is woven in crimson and two-tone gold. The classical design elements of a floral medallion with acanthus leaves was very fashionable during the Empire period. The piece is labelled 'pon 69840 Empire Armchair, brocade of 2 gold threads on crimson satin' and stamped with a CF logo, signifying that the piece belonged to Cartier et Fils.

We believe that the production of this piece was undertaken by Grand Frères for a prestigious client, possibly the Imperial court. This fabric was re-woven at a later date, as shown in the Tassinari et Chatel weaving production logs. The sett of the warp threads is dense and the execution of the weaving is of the highest quality. The cloth may have been commissioned by Cartier et Fils to Grand Frères or the stamped CF logo could just be the registering of the sample in the Cartier et Fils archive.

During the 1960s Tassinari et Chatel, who succeeded Grand Frères in 1871, re-wove this design in a blue colourway for chairs in the White House in Washington DC for the Kennedy Administration.

11 | ***Green Stool Covers with Crown of Roses***
French, Lyon, originally designed by Jacques-Louis de la Hamayde de Saint-Ange and manufactured by Seriziat & Cie for the Emperor's private room (cabinet de repos) at Versailles, 1813
93 × 67.5 cm (36 ½ × 26 ½ in)
Brocaded silk lampas

A floral design with central rosette motif on a green ground, designed by Saint-Ange, and intended to cover a pair of stools or chair seat and back, originally intended for Versailles. However, this fabric and its companion wall hanging were never installed during the Empire period but were later used in 1835 in the White Drawing Room at Fontainebleau for Queen Marie-Amelie. A silk of identical design to ours, but with attached floral border, is at Malmaison (MM40.47.3181). This was exhibited in *Soies tissées, soies brodées chez L'impératrice Joséphine*, held at Malmaison et Bois-Preau, 2002–03, no. 14a. The piece is also illustrated in Dumonthier, E. (1909a), pl. 60.

We do not know whether our silk was part of this original Imperial commission for Versailles as this design and similar patterns were also supplied to other important clients during the Restauration period. A slight variation of this example was supplied to the Prince Regent as stool coverings for Brighton Pavillion sometime between 1815 and 1820.

12 | *Centurion Helmets*

French, Lyon, probably manufactured by Bissardon,
Cousin et Bony, c1811
109 × 56 cm (43 × 22 in)
Brocaded metal and silver thread liseré on silk
taffeta ground

A striking silk faille, brocaded with metal thread
with a high silver content (75%), depicting two
centurion helmets, each within a diamond frame.
Similar designs to ours were first produced in
1811 by Bissardon, Cousin et Bony of Lyon for
upholstery in a number of different apartments
in Versailles. Seat covers, also with centurion
helmets, were supplied by Flamand in Paris for
the Prince Souverain in Fontainebleau in 1811.
Variations of this imperial design featuring the
centurion helmet were also produced, and ours is
one such variation.

The label attached to our silk states *'Faille 55
blue (12,120/21/22) brochée or Casques Empire 1m10'.*
The label reveals that this was one of a set of
covers, which was woven with the best silk yarn,
combined with a metal and 75% silver thread.
In 1811 the Emperor Napoleon commissioned
Bissardon, Cousin et Bony to weave and embroider
a series of silks for the palaces of Versailles and
Fontainebleau. They did this until 1812 when the
funds for these projects ceased.

13 | ***Urn with Floral Surround***
French, Lyon, probably manufactured by Chuard et Cie, 1811–20
88 × 54 cm (34 ½ × 21 ¼ in)
Silk lampas

An urn in a diamond-shaped floral surround, with a further leaf trail framing the central motif. The decoration is very finely drawn in yellow on a pale blue ground. Although we have not been able to identify this particular silk, similar blue and yellow damasks woven for the Imperial court by Chuard et Cie are published in Coural, J. (1980), pp. 225–26, and Gaudry, E. (1982), p. 53.

These were woven for the Emperor's Second Salon at Versailles by Chuard et Cie in 1811–12 (GMMP 1047/1). The identical design in a different colourway was commissioned for the Second Salon of the Empress at Versailles (GMMP 1270). These damasks were never actually installed in Versailles during the Empire period but, later, during the Restauration. The blue and yellow damasks were hung at the Elysée Palace for the Duc de Berry in 1816 where they remained until 1872 (Coural, J. (1980), pp. 227–28).

Chuard were Lyon manufacturers who wove for the Imperial court between 1811 and 1813. The were commissioned, along with Corderier et Lemire, to weave cloths for Versailles and the Grand Trianon. They had great exposure at the 1819 *Exposition des Produits de L'Industrie* and eventually, in 1830, they went into business with Corderier et Lemire becoming Corderier-Lemire and Chaurd et Cie. Chuard was eventually absorbed by Lemire.

14 | **_Seat and Sofa Covers_**
French, probably Lyon manufacturer, woven for
Cartier et Fils 1815–30
97 × 56 cm (38 × 22 in) chair seat and back
130 × 55 cm (51 × 21 ½ in) settee cover
Silk liseré

Two silk samples, one for a settee and another
for a chair bearing the motif of the seat and chair
back. The pattern features a central medallion
surrounded by quatrefoils and leaves, woven in red
silk with the pattern depicted in golden yellow silk,
the red ground woven with an all-over star pattern.
The silks are labelled and stamped with the logo
CF (Cartier et Fils). The label states 'G.R.H. & Cie
(George René Hamot & Co) No: 13046, Easy chair
fabric, crimson and yellow'.
   A very similar example woven in a blue and
gold silk is held in the Mobilier National and
published in Dumonthier, E. (1909a), p. 61. This silk
was supplied by Cartier et Fils to the court of either
Louis XVIII or Charles X between 1815 and 1830 for
one of the royal palaces.

15 | **_Chair Cover_**
French, Lyon manufacturer, for Cartier et Fils,
1814–30
115 × 60 cm (45 × 23 ½ in)
Silk liseré

A yellow and cream coloured silk liseré intended
for a chair back and seat. The piece is decorated
with a floral medallion and leaf surround for the
seat cover, identical in design to an earlier, Empire
silk (**cat no 10**). The cloth also has a smaller motif
of a leaf and central floral pattern for the back of the
chair. The size of the seat back motif is significantly
smaller than the previous Empire model, where the
image fills the frame of the seat back.
   In the Restauration period (1814–30) Empire-
style silks continued to be fashionable but the
designs became smaller in scale leaving a greater
area of plain background.
   We believe that our piece, which came from
the Hamot archive, was probably woven by one of
the distinguished Lyonnais firms, such as Grand
Frères, Chuard or Seguin, and sold through the silk
merchant Cartier et Fils.

16 | *Marguerites, Roses and Tulips*

French, probably Lyon manufacturer, designed by
Jacques-Louis de la Hamayde de Saint-Ange for
Charles X, 1824–30
124 × 60.5 cm (49 × 23 ¾ in)
Brocaded silk cannetillé

A chair fabric for both the seat and chair back,
depicting tulips, marguerites and roses surrounded
by a cartouche of yellow acanthus leaves,
sunflowers and red tulips on a pale blue cannetillé
ground. The design was produced by Saint-Ange,
who produced many furnishing designs for the
royal palaces of Charles X. The original design by
Saint-Ange was part of an album of designs sold at
auction in France in 1999 and is now in the Mobilier
National. Our silk is in the same colourway as the
painted design and is typical of the less formal,
lighter and more comfortable style of decoration at
the French court during this period.

The attached label states 'No: 2143, Cannetillé
61, blue brocade, Empire'. The cloth is also stamped
with the number 2143 and has the CF (Cartier et Fils)
stamp at the back of the cloth. The fabric was
acquired from the Hamot Collection, whose firm
took on the orders from the silk merchant Cartier
et Fils.

17 | ***Bed Canopy or Wall Covering***
French, unknown manufacturer, c1815–30
328 × 178 cm (129 × 70 in) canopy
327 × 33 cm (128 ½ × 13 in) border two pieces
Stencilled wall hanging with design of a star with
a diamond lattice and hand-painted border on a
moiré silk, in metallic pigment and pink paint

A large bed canopy or wall covering, made from
very fine moiré silk, the central field decorated
with an overall diamond lattice enclosing a floral
star, stencilled in a copper metallic pigment
and bordered on both sides with a hand-painted
scrolling floral and acanthus design in gold on a
pink ground. A separate border, similarly hand
painted with gold scrolling flowers and acanthus
leaves on pink, is edged with an egg and dart and
lattice border.

Such pieces were used either for the interior
section of bed canopies with the border featuring on
both the inside and the outside edge of the canopy.
Alternatively, they would have been used as wall
coverings within architectural wall mouldings. The
fabric would be stretched onto a frame and then
fixed to the wall; to hide the fixings the border was
then tacked on top of the cloth around the edge of
the frame. These stencilled silks were very fine but
fragile and are now extremely rare.

We have dated this piece to the Restauration
period, because there was then a fashion for
such painted effects on very fine silk for interior
decoration (Praz, M. (1964), p. 202). Our piece has
come from a private estate in France. This style
and technique continued into the Second Empire
as evidenced in a photograph (in Walton, W. (1992),
pl. 16) of a r oom in the Bibliothèque des Arts
Décoratifs in Paris.

18 | ***Chair and Sofa Seat Coverings***
French, unknown manufacturer, 1828–40
162 × 55 cm (63 × 21½ in)
Silk liseré

A series of blue and white silk panels for a suite
of furniture. These pieces consist of five chair
and seat back coverings and a sofa seat and back
covering. The pattern for the seat cushion is of a
floral central motif surrounded by a wide wreath
border; the seat back features a palmette with
the same wide wreath border. The sofa has the
same central floral motif, with acanthus leaves at
either side and a palmette composition similar to
the chair covers. These finely woven ice blue and
darker blue silks are remarkably detailed in their
pattern, including shadow-effect weaving within
the white design.

Some of the pieces have the number 1966
stamped on the back. This number could be either
the number for the client or the manufacturer
number. We have dated the silks to the end of the
reign of Charles X 1828–40, based on a brief fashion
at the time for a slightly larger scale motif, than
those which were produced in the early Resturation
period which were reduced in size to create a
larger background area. For example, compare
these silks with those used for a seat and sofa cover
(**cat no 14**) and with the earlier Empire period
furnishing silks (**cat no. 10**) where the design is
much larger. Similar examples of both period silks
are in the Wallace Collection in London.

Cat. 18

Cat. 18

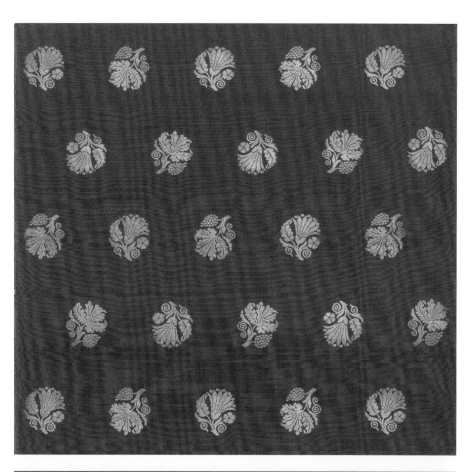

French, Lyon manufacturer, 1815–20
a) 58 × 54.5 cm (23 × 21 ½ in), brocaded silk and metal thread cannetillé
b) 53 × 56 cm (21 × 22 in), brocaded silk and metal thread taffeta

Two silk samples of a brocaded silk cannetillé and brocaded taffeta, both with the same type of design but of differing scales. These samples are brocaded in gold with a sprig of leaves and bell-shaped flowers. One of the samples has the label attached 'No: 2146 (Cannetillé) green P4 brocade 2 golds in a series of palms and small bell flowers, Empire'.

Although this style of decoration was popular during the Empire period, it continued to be used during the Restauration.

The design of our sample is similar in look to the silk drape linings (*pou de soie blanc broché deux ors*) woven by Bony for the blue velvet and gold bed hangings made for Louis XVIII, who died in 1824. These sumptuous hangings were then re-used for Charles X's bed in 1825, which is now in the Louvre (Coural, C. (2002b), pp. 64–65).

Silk in the Style of Daniel Marot
French, Lyon, manufactured by Grand Frères for
William Williams Hope, 1841
200 × 62 cm (79 × 24 ½ in)
Brocaded silk damask

A spectacular furnishing silk in crimson satin with
damask details, brocaded in golden yellow silk
featuring a wide band of interlinking strapwork
which runs vertically, loosely inspired by the
work of Daniel Marot (1661–1752). The design
repeat consists of a large escutcheon enclosing a
curved acanthus leaf, shaped into a pomegranate,
surrounded by *rinceaux* and curling tendrils and
a smaller, ogival motif with acanthus leaves at its
centre from which scrolling tendrils creep out to
the sides of the cloth.
On the back of the silk 'GRAND FRÈRES and TC' is
stamped and '1783' is written. There are two labels,
both with the number 1783. The second label also
bears the initials DB. The Tassinari et Chatel
archives list 1783 as a *'Damas Double Corps fond
Cramoisi broché ... fait en 1841 pour Mr Hope'*.

This silk was woven by Grand Frères in 1841
for the Hôtel de Monaco in Paris, now known
as the Hôtel de Sagan, residence of William
Williams Hope from 1838 until his death in 1855.
This Palladian style palace was originally built
for the Princess of Monaco, Marie-Catherine
de Brignole, in 1772 by Alexandre-Theodore
Brongniart. It passed through several hands before
being acquired by the fabulously rich William
Williams Hope in 1838. He commissioned the
architect Achille-Jacques Fedel (1785–1860) to
make both structural alterations and additions
and to undertake a complete renovation of the
interior using both Versailles and the Palais
Royal as inspiration. The general effect was one
of great opulence which served as a backdrop to
his magnificent art collection. Today, the Hôtel de
Sagan is the Polish Embassy.

A velvet of similar design to our silk was
woven by Lemire père et fils in 1865 for another
wealthy client of the time – the great courtesan of
the nineteenth century, La Païva, for her palatial
residence on the Champs-Elysées in Paris. This
was woven by Lemire père et fils as a ciselé velvet
and is illustrated in Verzier, P. (1998) p. 120. This
Lemire pattern was taken directly from an earlier
eighteenth-century silk lampas which had been
upholstered onto chairs for the Earl of Hope's seat
at Hopetoun House in Scotland. Lemire replaced
the existing design with another brightly coloured
silk during the 1850s. Hope's bedroom at the Hôtel
de Sagan, with its ornate furniture and furnishings,
has now been installed in the Musée des Arts
Décoratifs in Paris.

William Williams Hope (1802–1855)

Hope was born into a wealthy family. By the age
of eleven his father had died and left him a vast
fortune. At the age of twenty-six he bought Rushton
Hall in Northamptonshire for £140,000; however,
he seldom lived there, choosing to live at his home
in Amsterdam or Paris. During the mid-nineteenth

century Hope was one of the wealthiest men in the world; his business was banking, with the firm Hope & Co, as well as diamond merchanting (it was the Hope family who acquired the famous Hope Diamond in 1824). Hope was an eccentric, who spoke English with a foreign accent and had his shirts sent to England to be laundered. He was known to have lavish parties but if he was crossed he would seek retribution. A letter to his land agent based in Berkeley Square, London, tells of how he bought one of his courtesans a very expensive necklace, but when he discovered her affair with another man, he called for it to be cleaned. A month later the jeweller called on the lady asking her to pay the bill. Hope had asked the jeweller to replace the real diamonds for fakes. Hope remained a bachelor but was very much admired and had many lady friends. He died leaving his fortune between the steward of the Rushton estate and three ladies of Paris, one of whom he had an association with for 18 years. When one of them disputed the will, the court decided that she was allowed the use of his coach and horses for only one day.

21,22 Alhambra

French, Lyon, design after Owen Jones, probably manufactured by Mathevon et Bouvard, 1866–80
192 × 54.5 cm (75 × 21 in) red colourway
150 × 54.5 cm (59 × 21 in) blue colourway
Brocaded lampas

Two striking designs, one in a red colourway with details in blue, golden yellow and dark green and another in a blue colourway with details in red and green and again with gold-coloured strapwork features.

The silks are inspired by Spanish Nasrid decoration, in particular the Moorish palace, the Alhambra, in Granada. From the early 1830s there began a series of publications which featured detailed architectural drawings of this magnificent palace. The first was produced by the Frenchman Joseph Pierre Girault de Pragney, followed by Pascal-Xavier Coste, and then in 1842, Owen Jones along with Jules Goury published *Plans, Elevations, Sections and Details of the Alhambra*. This was a two-volume publication of which the second volume detailed the flat plates of the stone, and stucco work of the walls, columns and arches within the palace. In the case of this design the inspiration came from an amalgam of designs from this Moorish palace. Some of the scrollwork pattern elements of this silk can be seen in all these publications as well as the later printing of the 1856 *The Grammar of Ornament*, again composed and written by the architect Owen Jones. The publication looked at design from many different cultures. These books influenced many areas of the decorative arts throughout Europe, including silk weaving.

Similar examples to our silks were produced by Mathevon et Bouvard and are now in the Musée des Arts Décoratifs in Paris and are illustrated in LeClercq, J-P. (2004), p. 109. An analysis of the weaving structure shows a significant number of threads in the warp, called ends per inch. Our silks were compared with other known existing Mathevon et Bouvard examples in both Lyon and Paris and we found the same technical weaving structure in these too. British trade journals of the time state that Mathevon were one of a very few French companies that had the equipment and technical ability to weave more than 800 ends per inch for a silk cloth. The successors to Mathevon et Bouvard, Bucol, have a very small silk fragment in their archive which bears strong similarities to sections of our design. Our silks come from the estate of George and René Hamot, who were also active collectors of work from the House of Mathevon et Bouvard.

23 | Alhambra

French, Lyon, probably manufactured by Corderier
et Lemire or Mathevon et Bouvard, c1835–55
117 × 54.5 cm (46 × 21 in)
Silk lampas with yellow, blue and black
supplementary wefts on a red satin ground
Label stuck on the back of the silk reads 'number
3206 lampas red ground, Alhambra'

The Lyonnais textile industry supplied silks mainly
to the Ottoman and Persian courts throughout the
Restauration (1814–30) and the July Monarchy
(1830–48). Concurrently, there existed in France
a fashion for Orientalist decoration. The Duc
d'Orléans, son of Louis-Philippe, commissioned
Grand Frères to weave Moresque designs for his
private apartments in the Tuileries, which were
delivered in 1842. His brother, le Prince de Joinville,
also commissioned silks with Moorish designs in
the late 1830s and 1840s. An Islamic textile once
belonging to the Empress Josephine was lent
to Mathevon et Bouvard by the *Garde-Meuble* in
1837 to reweave into striped textiles 'a la turque'
for the Turkish salon of le Prince de Joinville in
the Tuileries. Other sources of inspiration came
from contemporary publications, such as Owen
Jones's *Plans, Elevations, Sections and Details of the
Alhambra* (1842) and his immensely influential *The
Grammar of Ornament*, first published in 1856 and
later, in French, in 1865. These showed a series of
studies that Jones undertook of the architecture
of various Islamic and Moorish buildings, in
particular the famous Alhambra, of Granada, in
southern Spain.

The tightly conceived design of our Alhambra
silk, together with its weaving peculiarities, such
as the dark shading within the architectural
elements throwing light and shade onto the design
produces an almost *trompe l'oeil* effect, which is
also present in another Alhambra silk (patron 3622)
woven by Corderier et Lemire as early as 1835 and
now in the Musée de la Mode et du Textile in Paris.

Similar pattern elements of this luxurious silk
can be seen in the later printing of Jones, O. (1868),
Arabian section no. 2. and p. 59 and the Moresque
section no. 3. Many firms used Jones's publication
as a source of inspiration and as such other similar
examples can be found to have been produced
by many European silk weaving mills. It is not
fully known whether Jones did actually design
this piece, as no documentary evidence exists to
confirm this. It is also believed that this design
could have been woven for a grand property, Hôtel
de Païva, owned by the Marquise de la Païva, a
very wealthy woman and a great courtesan of the
mid to late nineteenth century.

24 | **Mauresque**

French, Lyon, manufactured by Mathevon et
Bouvard for Ferdinand Duplan et Cie, 1856–70
165 × 60 cm (65 × 23 ½ in)
Brocaded silk lampas
Attached label stating 'F D & Cie no 11885' with
a smaller, gold-edged paper label of Mathevon et
Bouvard underneath

This silk sample decorated in yellow/gold on a
crimson ground was probably designed and woven
as a long cushion for an Orientalist room or a
Turkish salon which was fashionable in Paris in the
nineteenth century. The shape and general design
of this silk is inspired by Islamic textiles but the
individual motifs are a European interpretation.

The fabric features a central floral and scroll
section with stylised petal edges, and each petal
contains a floral sprig. At each end of this middle
section is a stylised flower where again the petal
and floral sprig is repeated around a flower centre.
The ground of the cloth is woven in a crimson

and red silk in an interlocking rectangular shape.
Various pattern elements of this piece were
inspired by study drawings undertaken by several
architects of the mid-nineteenth century and can be
seen in Coste, P. (1867), pl. 22; Girault de Pragney,
J. P. (1836–39), pl. 15; and Jones, O. and Goury, Jules
M. (1842), pl. 12.

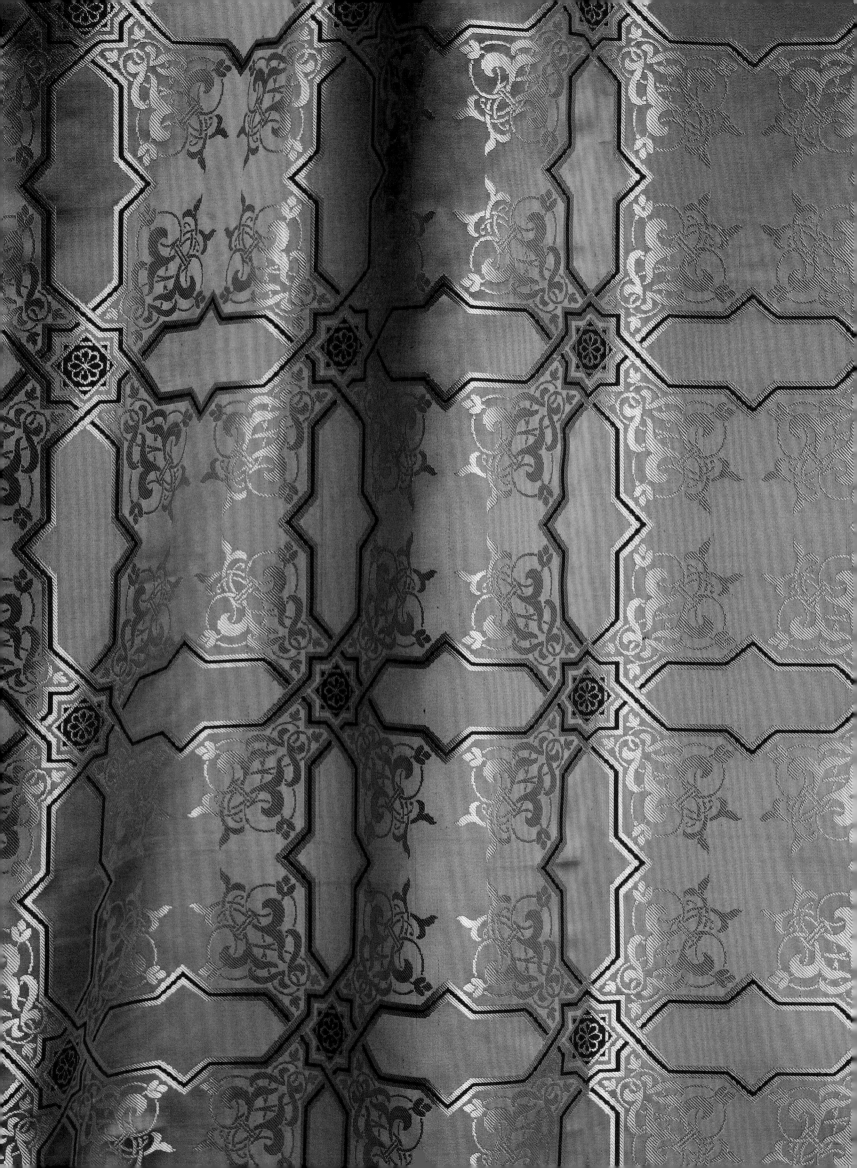

25 | Byzantine

French, Lyon, probably manufactured by Mathevon
et Bouvard, c1866–80
136 × 127 cm (53 ½ × 50 in), two pieces
Silk lampas

The design of this fabric, despite its title, is an
adaptation of design elements of decorative tile
work that was found in The Hall of Ambassadors
at the Alhambra and featured in Owen Jones's *The
Grammar of Ornament*, Moresque Design, no. 4, pl.
XLIII, first published in 1856 and also the *Plans,
Elevations, Sections and Details of the Alhambra, Vol.
II*, pl. 10, printed in 1842. These books were and are
so influential that Islamic designs adapted from
Jones's line drawings provided many industrial
manufacturers throughout Europe with ideas and
inspiration for all areas of the decorative arts,
including cloth, from the mid-1850s until the late
1880s.

Although Jones was the most famous 'translator'
of this style, the Frenchman Girault de Pragney
also undertook detailed drawings of the buildings,
stonework and ornamentation and again design
elements too can be found in his publication
(Girault de Pragney, J. P. (1842), pl. 15 and pl. 27).

The silk features an octagon shape, which
has scroll and filigree work at each corner of the
octagon and a smaller red and gold outlined star
with a floral centre motif. The piece is woven in a
brilliant blue with red and gold colours. The fabric
is a fine silk lampas weaving and bears the label
'blue & red, no F1022 (pon: 4205) Lampas 130 of
blue and gold "Byzantine"'. The fabric would have
been used for curtaining as well as for upholstery.
Islamic-inspired designs became popular during
the mid-nineteenth century and ran alongside the
other popular design style, Neo-Gothic.

26 | ***Stripe in the style of 'Gilet Persan'***
French, Lyon, probably manufactured by Mathevon et Bouvard, for Ferdinand Duplan et Cie, c1840
133 × 56.5 cm (52 × 22 ¼ in)
Silk, cotton and metal liseré

A pretty diagonal stripe, probably copying a Persian fabric for costume. The fabric is woven in a diagonal blue and gold stripe featuring a small flower trail stripe with a bud and leaf scroll on the right-hand side of the stripe. These petite dimity designs were often originally used for dress fabrics. They were then translated into a heavier, furnishing fabric to be used as either linings, curtains, wall panels, portieres or to cover a divan or cushions in an Ottoman or Orientalist salon ('salon turc'), which was then *de rigueur* in fashionable Paris. For example, the Duc d'Orléans had a richly decorated brocatelle in a Moresque design in his grand salon at the Tuileries Palace in 1841 and, in 1837-38, le Prince de Joinville commissioned Mathevon et Bouvard to copy an original Turkish striped fabric, once belonging to Josephine Bonaparte, for his 'salon turc' at the Tuileries.

This type of design continued to be fashionable throughout the nineteenth century as can be seen in silk manufacturers' log books, samples of which are featured in Coural, C. (2002b), pp. 78-79.

The sample has a label with the words 'FD&Co no 5477, silk and gold brocade'. FD&Co stands for the firm Ferdinand et Duplan, a well-known Parisian silk merchant.

27 | ***Turkish-inspired stripe***
French, Lyon manufacturer, for Ferdinand Duplan et Cie, c1840
68.5 × 56.5 cm (27 × 22 ¼ in)
Brocaded cotton, metal and silk liseré

An Ottoman-inspired striped fabric, probably sourced from dress fabric. This delicate design depicts bands of meandering floral decoration on a gold ground bordered in blue and gold, alternating with bands of puce decorated with a repeating gold motif.

Together with our other example (**cat no 26**) as well as other striped silks 'a la turque', such as those woven for le Prince de Joinville for his Turkish salon in the Tuileries Palace, these furnishing fabrics were fashionable in Paris as divan or cushion covers, wall coverings or curtains in specially designed Orientalist rooms.

According to the historian Florence Charpigny, a similarly coloured sample dating from 1840 is in the Conseil des Prud'hommes archive in Lyon.

The attached label bears the stamp of F. D. & Co (for Ferdinand, Duplan et Cie) with the manufacturer's number 5478 and patron number 707.

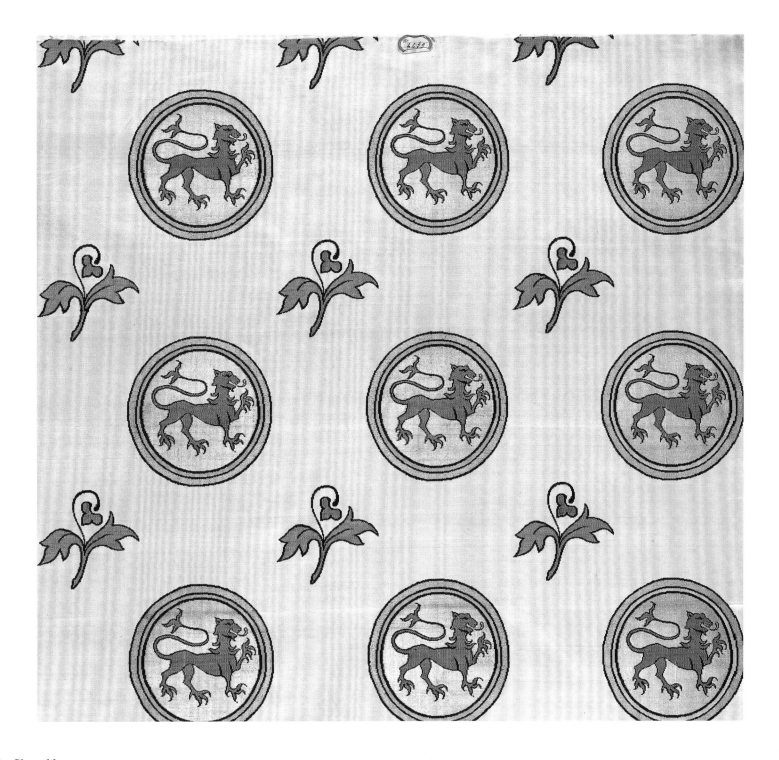

28   *Silk for Chasuble*

French, Lyon, designed by Eugène Viollet-le-Duc, manufactured by Lemire père et fils for the 1855 Paris Exposition Universelle
61 × 56 cm (24 × 22 ¼ in)
Silk lampas brocaded with gold, silver and silk on a satin ground

This silk brocade was first woven by the firm Lemire père et fils for the Exposition Universelle held in Paris in 1855. The fabric features a floral sprig with the heraldic symbol of a lion in the passant stance woven in purple silk within a silver circle edged with a gold border. The silk was used as the ground cloth for a chasuble, which was illustrated in the contemporary literature (Lasteyrie, de, F. and Darcet, A. (1855), pp. 339 and 389). This publication referred to the fabric as remarkable. Ferdinand de Lasteyrie wrote 'we have especially noticed, and admired a white fabric chasuble, which bears drawing and form

that recalls the better models of the XII and XIII centuries', while Alfred Darcet mentions '…from MM Lemire and Sons there is a chasuble of white damask that is decorated with circles of silver with a purple ring surround, and purple lions at the centre'.

The piece is labelled with a small paper disc with number 4473. This label is the manufacturing number for Lemire, the firm which was subsequently taken over by Prelle and the piece is stamped LYON on the back. The record sample log book and illustration of the chasuble are published in Valentin, F. (2003), pp. 136–38, and were also included in the exhibition at the Musée Carnavalet in Paris from November 2002 to February 2003, which commemorated the 250th anniversary of the silk weaving firms now owned by Prelle.

Viollet-le-Duc (1814–1879) was a French architect, antiquarian and designer who based his work on a profound knowledge of Medieval

buildings, which he believed provided a basis for a new, contemporary philosophy of design. He was highly influential in his time and wrote two large works – *Dictionnaire raisonné de l'architecture française du XI au XVI siècle* (ten vols 1858–68) and its companion *Dictionnaire du mobilier français de l'époque carlovingienne à la Rénaissance* (six vols 1858–75). Like Pugin in England, he was a distinguished proponent of the Neo-Gothic style in France through his architecture and also his furniture and interiors, which were all conceived in the Gothic style. This well-known silk is an excellent example of the taste for Medieval design in France and elsewhere in Europe at this time.

29 | Rosaces
French, unknown manufacturer, 1850–65
274 × 55 cm (29 × 21 ½ in)
Silk brocatelle

A co-ordinating fabric sample woven in emerald green and gold, the pattern is a stylised rose motif with a fleur-de-lys insert to each petal. Each flower is linked by a thin gold line, which has in the middle of it a smaller floral element. The stylised design of this motif is that of the Neo-Gothic style where its revival became popular during the mid-nineteenth century. The piece bears the paper label featuring a moth and mulberry branch logo and is written 'Brocatelle of green and gold with rose motif'.

Brocatelle silk samples, which are hard wearing, were often used for upholstery on deep-buttoned back chairs or sofas.

30 | St Louis
French, unknown manufacturer, 1850–65
61 × 55 cm (24 × 21 ½ in)
Silk brocatelle

A Neo-Gothic textile consisting of an interlacing lattice across the whole of the cloth, where inside the diamond sections of the lattice there appear circular medallions. Within each section is a fleur-de-lys motif which points outwards; a smaller fleur-de-lys figuring is then repeated in four other sections of the lattice and points inwards. Two shades of green are used and the cloth is woven in a brocatelle structure. The cloth has a paper label attached, which states 'Brocatelle 55, 3 greens, "St Louis"'. The piece was intended to be used as upholstery cloth or possibly for ecclesastical use.

St Louis probably refers to Saint Louis, King Louis IX of France (r. 1226–1270). The fleur-de-lys, a stylised iris flower, was adopted by the French monarchy as their heraldic symbol but it was never officially used during the French Republics.

French, Lyon, manufactured by Grand Frères for
Cartier et Fils, c1850
68 × 54.5 cm (26 ¾ × 21 ½ in)
Silk brocatelle

A mid-nineteenth century Renaissance-inspired
silk brocatelle which depicts an interlacing
strapwork with a stylised floral and filigree central
motif. Woven in a crimson and gold silk, the
piece bears a paper label featuring the moth and
mulberry branch motif which states 'Brocatelle 55
crimson and gold Renaissance'. At the top right
corner of the fabric is the CF stamp for the silk
merchant Cartier et Fils.
This silk was originally woven by Grand Frères
for Cartier. This research was documented in the
Tassinari et Chatel archives no. 4406, where we
discovered that Tassinari et Chatel, successors to
Grand Frères, re-wove this design as a silk lampas
for a Mr J. B. Ang in 1919.

32 | **Sainte Chapelle**

French, Lyon, probably manufactured by Mathevon
et Bouvard for Cartier et Fils, c1865
88 × 54.5 cm (34 ¾ × 21 ½ in)
Silk brocatelle

A furnishing fabric decorated with a lozenge-
shaped strapwork with quatrefoil elements and leaf
trail central motif, woven as a brilliant burgundy
and gold brocatelle. The attached paper label
states 'pon: 851, Brocatelle of garnet and gold Ste
Chapelle' and the silk also bears the stamped mark
of CF for Cartier et Fils.

An almost identical silk brocatelle, also entitled
'Brocatelle Sainte Chapelle', was probably woven
by Mathevon et Bouvard in 1865, according to
LeClercq, J-P. (2004), no. 72, p. 110. He compares the
design to an example in the Mathevon et Bouvard
(Bucol) archive numbered 8340. Thierry Mieg, the
print manufacturer, also produced exactly the same
design as ours but as a block-printed burgundy
chintz, which was produced between 1850 and
1880. The design for this printed chintz is in the
Musée de L'Impression sur l'Étoffes in Mulhouse
no. 1171/7.

The source of inspiration for these textiles
almost certainly came from a lithograph published
in Decloux and Doury (1865), pl. 7, no. 4, *decoration
d'une colonne rouge du jube, grandeur d'execution*.
The Sainte Chapelle in Paris is a reliquary shrine
built by King Louis to house the holy relics brought
back from the Crusade in 1240.

The Neo-Gothic style in France in the mid-
nineteenth century took its inspiration from a
revival of interest in the design and conservation
of Medieval architecture, murals and paintings.
Similar Neo-Gothic designs were woven in England
by Norris & Co and Crace & Co from the late 1840s
onwards for Victorian interiors of which the Palace
of Westminster was the most famous.

33 | *Neo-Gothic Shop Display Blind*
French, in the style of Eugène Viollet-le-Duc, for
the shop Savary in Paris, c1865
220 × 102.5 cm (86 ½ × 44 ¼ in)
Cotton canvas, hand painted and stencilled

A hand-painted and stencilled shop display blind,
produced for the shop Savary, which sold luxury
goods such as porcelain, Limoges ware and other
decorative items, comparable to the British shop
Thomas Goode. How the blind was used is not
known, although it is thought that it would have
featured in a display.

The image on the blind is inspired from a
thirteenth-century stained-glass window and is
very similar to a drawing by the French architect
Eugène Viollet-le-Duc (illustrated in Decloux and
Doury (1865), pl. 17). The Neo-Gothic style appeared
in many decorative art disciplines and was very
popular during the mid-nineteenth century.

The pair to this blind is now in the Royal
Museums of Scotland in Edinburgh.

Stamped at the bottom left along the blue border
are the words: 'Savary Rue de Bolles'.

34 | ***Floral Spray***
French, Lyon, probably manufactured by Grand
Frères for Cartier et Fils, 1850–60
163 × 54.5 cm (64 × 21 ½ in)
Brocaded silk lampas

A floral spray with feathers and flowers is finely
woven as a brocaded silk lampas in metal and
silk. The silk lampas is a mid-nineteenth century
re-weave of an earlier eighteenth-century Rococo
point-rentré pattern, made for dress. These
historical revival designs proved popular in the
Napoleon III period when they were used for
upholstery silk.

The piece is labelled with a parchment label
with the initials C. & F. (Cartier et Fils) 'No 17923
Pon 638, lampas rose & argent' and comes from the
Tassinari et Chatel archive. Our piece is illustrated
in Schoeser, M. (2007), p. 116.

| **Faisan Doré (Golden Pheasant)**
French, Lyon, manufactured by Grand Frères,
1865–70
142 × 45 cm (56 × 17 ¾ in)
| Brocaded silk lampas

This grand design was woven by Grand Frères
up to 1870 and then by Tassinari et Chatel from
1871 until the mid-twentieth century. The design
features two central motifs of a proud pair of golden
pheasants and a floral bouquet. Both motifs are
surrounded by a damask of Baroque acanthus leaf
scrollwork and floral trail with two putti swathed
in cloth supporting an escutcheon and caryatids
at either selvedge. The pattern is thus placed so
that the silk can be used as either wall hangings or
as upholstery seating. It lends itself to the grand
interior settings of the *nouveaux riches*. The cloth
employs the use of the newly discovered Perkins
purple, which was invented in 1856, as well as the
old method of silk dyed from cochineal.

This design had a transatlantic appeal and
was supplied to the American furnishing house
F. Schumacher in the early part of the twentieth
century. At that time, Schumacher sold this silk for
$54 a piece, an astronomical price intended for the
wealthy American elite. Our piece is illustrated in
Schoeser, M. (2007), p. 121, with the Schumacher
piece being illustrated in Slavin, R. (1992), pl. 54.
The Tassinari et Chatel archive log books records
the number 2781 as having been woven before 1870,
by Grand Frères. The label attached to our cloth
states 'Lampas 55 of garnet [sic] brocaded golden
pheasant pon (patron) 2781'.

| *Floral Bouquet in the Louis XVI style*
French, Lyon, designed and commissioned by
Grande Barbe, manufactured by Grand Frères, 1863
356 × 67 cm (142 × 26 ¼ in)
| Brocaded silk lampas

An imposing and long length of furnishing fabric
with a large repeat featuring two colourful floral
bouquets in ornamental urns, surrounded by
rinceaux, garlands of flowers and strings of pearls,
all woven in a silvery white silk on a deep red
ground. A cameo hangs from one of the bouquets
of flowers. At either selvedge is a floral posy and
next to the large urn is a trophy of a lit torch, quill
and arrows with a hunting horn. The piece is made
dramatic by the stark contrast of the brightly
coloured bouquets against the white patterning of
the other design features.
The Tassinari et Chatel archives note that this
silk design (no. 2095 in their order books) was
conceived ('composé pour nous') by Monsieur
Grandbarbe (sic) in the Louis XVI style and
prepared for weaving in November 1863. The label
attached to the piece states the manufacturer
number 53652 and the pattern number 2095.

The Louis XVI and other decorative styles were
popular during the Second Empire when it was
fashionable to look stylistically to the past for
inspiration. The Tassinari et Chatel records show

that the cloth was woven for the interior decorating firm Grande Barbe. They provided an artistic service of supplying *nouveaux riches* clients with matching bespoke furnishings, wallpapers and furniture. In some cases they provided their own designs to be woven to order and they contracted their weaving to the best mills in Europe, including Keith & Co from England and Grand Frères in France.

Rinceaux is originally a French term describing a linear arrangement of spiralling scrolls of foliage where the scrolls alternate from clockwise to anti-clockwise.

37 | Les Saltimbanques (The Acrobats)
French, Lyon, probably designed by Arthur Martin, manufactured by Grand Frères, 1868
148 × 55 cm (48 ¼ × 21 ¼ in)
Silk lampas

A dramatic silk lampas in a deep burgundy, the pattern finely woven in shades of white, featuring two central motifs, surrounded by scrolling *rinceaux* and floral and pearl garlands. The first motif features two acrobats, one dressed as a jester and the other, a lady dressed in theatrical period costume, playing a tambourine. From the plinth on which they dance hangs a tasselled canopy over a trophy of a theatrical mask, a trumpet and a dagger. The central figures are heralded by three putti. The second register is a floral bouquet of roses and peonies placed on an ornamental plinth of *rinceaux* and a cameo from which falls a floral and pearl garland.

The style and execution of this silk is extremely close to The Performers (**cat no 38**), which has been ascribed to Arthur Martin in the Tassinari et Chatel log books. Our silk is labelled with the manufacturer numbers 4198 and 6981 in addition to a wax seal with the initials DBB. Les Saltimbanques is stamped on the back with TC (logo of Tassinari et Chatel who were the successors to Grand Frères, taking over the good will and order book of the firm in 1870). The Tassinari et Chatel archives identify the date of weaving of our silk to 20 March 1868.

38 | **_The Performers_**
French, Lyon, designed by Arthur Martin in August 1867, prepared for weaving by Monsieur Vigouroux, manufactured by Grand Frères
151 × 54.5 cm (59 × 21 in)
Silk cannetillé lampas

An impressive silk lampas woven in a bright yellow silk with a pale and emerald green silk being used for the design. The textile features two central registers, surrounded by scrolling _rinceaux_, putti with musical instruments and floral garlands. Two theatrical performers are on a plinth, one playing the tambourine, the other dancing, both with a goose in attendance. Below the plinth is a palmette with a grotesque feature from which spreads a tasselled canopy with a floral wreath. The second register is an asymmetrical bouquet of roses and peonies which is placed on a scrolling leaf plinth. Hanging from this scrollwork is a trophy of a tambourine with two mock sceptres of a puppet head on each end.

The design by Arthur Martin is inspired by different seventeenth- and eighteenth-century design elements. The performers, in particular the dancing figure, relate to a costume opera design by Jean Bérain whereas the putti and floral elements mirror eighteenth-century patterns. Our silk is labelled with the manufacturer numbers 2143 and 6973. The Tassinari et Chatel production log books describe pattern 2143 as _'Lampas Louis XV, fait pour nous en Aout 1867 par Monsieur Arthur Martin d'apres des dessein J Bérain – mis en carte sur 800 cordes reduction par Ms Vigouroux…'._

39 | **_Renaissance-style Lampas_**
French, Lyon, designed and prepared for weaving by Louis Roux for Grand Frères in February 1869
210 × 129 cm (83 ¾ × 50 ¾ in)
Silk lampas

A large width of dramatic silk, which is very ornate, featuring parallel columns of decoration in tones of beige/brown and crimson against a royal purple ground, designed by Louis Roux in what he perceived to be the Louis XIII style. Louis XIII reigned from 1601 to 1643.

The hanging features a broad vertical strapwork design, like a pilaster, of ornamental plasterwork of palmettes, canopies, grotesques, parrots and mythical animals which frame two bouquets of flowers. In the centre, against the violet ground, a smaller bouquet is held by a scallop shell from which falls a tasselled canopy held between the mouths of the two griffins.

Tassinari et Chatel log books state patron 2163 _'Lampas 2 lattes sur un fond en deux couleurs dessin Louis XIII – des perroquets fait pour nous et mis en carte par Louis Roux en Fev 1869'._

40 | **Van Dyke**

French, Lyon, designed in 1869 by Monsieur Roux,
manufactured by Maison Prelle, and woven for
Marble House in Newport in 1890
a) 151 × 75 cm (59 × 29 ½ in)
b) 244 × 75 cm (96 × 29 ½ in)
Silk lampas

This grand fabric is designed in the style of Jean
Bérain, draughtsman, designer, painter and
engraver to the court of Louis XIV. The Bérain style
featured arabesques and elaborate grotesques.
Woven in two tones of red, it depicts an urn with
lion's feet filled with flowers under an elaborate
domed canopy and above a cupola from which
hangs a garland of flowers. Examples of the silk are
illustrated in Verzier P. (1998), p. 121.

The Prelle archives have a velvet woven to
commission on 16 September and 8 October 1869.
The design was re-woven in 1890 as a silk lampas
for Alva Vanderbilt's bedroom at her home,
Marble House, in Newport, Rhode Island, USA.
The room was decorated by Allard of Paris and
the house, designed by Richard Morris Hunt, was
built between 1888 and 1892 for William Kissam
Vanderbilt (1849-1920). The house features a
number of elaborate rooms, with ceiling murals,
chandeliers, carved and gilded woodwork, and a
grand staircase.

The Vanderbilt men were the merchant
princes of America because of their prominence
in business and the arts. William K. Vanderbilt
inherited a fortune of $60 million, which he
continued to invest primarily in the railroads. He
married Alva Erskine Smith in 1875 but the couple
divorced in 1897. Their daughter Consuela (1877-
1964) married the ninth Duke of Marlborough in
1895, living at Blenheim Palace in Oxfordshire.

41 | *Floral Lampas with Caryatids and Plumed Mascarons*
French, Lyon, designed by Arthur Martin and
manufactured by Grand Frères, 1870
136 × 73 cm (53 ¼ × 28¼ in)
Silk lampas

A dramatic silk, in tones of red copper, which was
designed by the Arthur Martin studio, inspired
by the Louis XIV style of decoration. The cloth
depicts two central motifs, which are surrounded
by ornamental *rinceaux*, palmettes, caryatids and
mascarons.

The first register is smaller in scale to the
second larger register; this is so that the cloth could
either be used to upholster furniture or applied as
wall covering. The smaller section would have been
used for a chair back with the larger being used for
the seat cover. The fabric is also woven to be used
as wall covering, where the two motifs are seen as
part of the length of the cloth. The features on the
mascarons and caryatids are exquisitely produced
and the tonal shades of the silk are used to denote
the expressions within the features.

Tassinari et Chatel production log books give
the name of the designer, the date of May 1870 and
the pattern number 2185. Attached to the silk is a
label with the numbers *'33079 and 2185 lampas …3
cuivres'* and Arthur Martin in pencil on the back of
the label.

42 | *Playful Putti*

French, Lyon, designed by Arthur Martin,
manufactured by Mathevon et Bouvard, 1873
180 × 75 cm (71 × 29 ½ in)
Brocaded silk lampas

A spectacular furnishing silk featuring greyish
blue putti playing musical instruments or holding
up baskets of colourful flowers. The putti are
surrounded by scrolling arabesque *rinceaux* and
ornamental features of mascarons, dolphins and
oriental urns.

These Belle Époque designs, which were inspired
by the plate engravings of Jean Bérain, were
produced by many Lyon firms such as Tassinari et
Chatel, Grand Frères, Lamy et Giraud and Prelle, and
Arthur Martin supplied designs to all of them.

A silk with similarly drawn putti was produced
for the Empress Eugénie and exhibited at the
Exposition Universelle of 1867, now in the Musée des
Tissus in Lyon and is illustrated Calavas, A. (1905),
pl. XXIV.

The design for this silk is also in the Musée des
Tissus in Lyon (no. 46525) and was exhibited by
Mathevon et Bouvard at the 1873 Vienna Exhibition.
The Art Institute of Chicago has a silk of this
design (1988.526) (Arizzoli-Clémentel, P. (1990),
p. 222; Soira, A. (2002), pp. 92–93; Thurman, C.
C. Mayer (1992), pp. 93 and 147; and Bouzard, M.
(1999), p. 63).

| *Velvet for Hôtel de la Païva*

French, Lyon, designed in 1873 for Hôtel de la
Païva, manufactured by Tassinari et Chatel
162 × 68.5 cm (63 ¾ × 26 ¾ in) brown and cream
139 × 69 cm (54 ¾ × 27 ¼ in) red and burgundy
Silk velvet ciselé (cut and uncut velvet)

A grandiose ciselé velvet, inspired by the
decorative elements of the Renaissance and
Baroque repertoire, particularly the designs of
Jean Bérain (1638–1711). This rich interpretation
of historical styles is typical of the unrestrained
lavishness favoured among the *nouveaux riches* of
Europe during the second half of the nineteenth
century. Velvets such as ours would have been
used to upholster furniture or as wall coverings.

These velvets have a large pattern repeat of
two addorsed sphinxes resting on plinths and
supporting a central mascaron below two sirens
who hold a large urn of flowers. Above, is a smaller
bouquet of flowers set between two dolphins and is
linked to an ornamental display. The 'Païva' velvets
are particularly refined due to their well-drawn
composition, the unusually high level of execution
and the subtle use of paler and darker hues of the
same colour.

The archives of Tassinari et Chatel reveal that
the brown and cream velvet panel was woven and
delivered on 5 April 1873. Both pieces are labelled
with the pattern number 4410 and the client
number. Several examples of this velvet are in the
Musée des Tissus in Lyon. The earliest example
(no. 26954) was woven in April 1873 and delivered
in 1874 to Monsieur Rival de Rouville, living at the
Place Bellecour in Lyon. We believe the velvet was
originally installed as wall covering within gilded
architectural frames in the main drawing room at
the Hôtel de Païva (Fregnac, C. and Andrews, W.
(1977), p. 238). The velvet is also illustrated in Soria,
A. (2002), p. 92; Arizzoli-Clémentel, P. (1990), p. 221;
Heutte, R. (1980), p. 93; Bouzard, M. (1999), p. 62;
and Marinis, F. (1994), p. 59.

This piece has had a long and noted production
history. Tassinari et Chatel and Prelle wove
the fabrics for the famous Hôtel de Païva, at 25
Champs-Elysées, Paris in 1865, 1866 and 1873.
The palace was built between 1855 and 1865 by
the architect Pierre Manguin and was one of the
most ostentatious and opulent *hôtels particuliers*
of its time. Paul Baudry, Jules Dalou and other
famous artists of the period fitted out the interior
in precious marbles, gold, bronze and mosaics in
unheard-of profusion. Lavish and splendid textiles
were woven by the foremost weaving houses of
Lyon – Tassinari et Chatel and Prelle. The palace
gained its notoriety from its owner, the Marquise
de Païva, who was one of the great courtesans of
the nineteenth century.

La Païva was born Esther Pauline Lachmann
(1819–1884); her parents were Jewish Polish
immigrants who lived in poverty in Moscow. At
the age of 17 she married a Russian tailor, Antione
Villoing, by whom she had a son. She fled her
marriage and family moving to Paris where she

assumed the name Thérèse Pauline Lachmann. Her intention was to amass her fortune, and this she did by using her prodigious powers of attraction. Her first rich suitor was Henri Herz, a pianist, through whom she gained access to many artists, musicians and writers of the time. She became Herz's mistress and it is said that they married in London, but this would have made her a bigamist and there is no proof of a marriage ever taking place. Her ferocious sexual appetite and methods of seduction saw her having affairs with Richard Wagner, Hans von Bülow and Théophile Gautier to name but a few. La Païva's spending almost ruined Herz, seeing her being banished from the Herz estate. She then took up residence at the Hôtel Valin, before moving to London. While in London she caught the attention of Lord Stanley who introduced her to the British aristocratic lifestyle which she had always craved. By now her first husband had died of consumption and so she was free to marry again. Stanley refused her suggestion of marriage and so she returned to Paris. While attending a spa at Baden she met Albino Francesco de Païva-Araujo, a Portuguese Marquis. It is said that she blackmailed him into marriage, marrying him on 5 June 1851, acquiring a title. The day after the wedding she rebuked her husband, by stating that they could not be seen in public because she was a prostitute and she had got from him what she wanted: a title and a position and that all her new husband wanted was a night of passion. Upon these words the Marquis returned to Portugal, where the marriage was finally annulled in 1871. It was from this marriage that she acquired the nickname La Païva.

Her final suitor and conquest was a Prussian Count, Guido Henckel von Donnersmarck; she married him in 1871 and it is he who financed the building and refurbishment of her opulent palace later named Hôtel Païva, based in Paris on the Champs-Elysées. The palace became famed for its portraits of her, its onyx staircase, ornate furnishings and elaborate bath, and is a significant example of the taste of the Second Empire. Her time at her palace was short and she and her husband were exiled on suspicion of espionage charges made by the French state. They fled to the family castle in Neudeck where she died in 1885; her husband had her body preserved in alcohol and he kept her body at his castle.

Bérainesque Moquette

French, Lyon, design attributed to Arthur Martin
Studio, manufactured by Mathevon et Bouvard,
c1875
147 × 70 cm (55 × 27½ in)
Cotton moquette

A brown moquette with a large design repeat
which features two registers. The larger of the
two depicts an ornamental urn between two putti
surrounded by rinceaux, small floral bouquets and
a palmette. Ornamental strapwork links this to the
other register showing an oriental figure in ornate
dress, an elaborate turban very much in the style
of Jean Bérain costume designs of around 1700. The
piece is named Asan and has the manufacturer
numbers of 209 / 4048.

Designs such as these became popular with
the revival of Renaissance and Baroque styles
during the third quarter of the nineteenth century.
Weaving firms such as Tassinari et Chatel, Grand
Frères, Prelle and Mathevon et Bouvard supplied
cloth such as this to wealthy clients around
the world. This piece would have been used for
upholstery and is likely to have fitted onto a high-
backed chair.

A moquette is a type of velvet which is
extremely hard-wearing, made of cotton or wool
or wool and cotton mix. The ground pile remains
uncut, producing a ribbed effect. The pattern can
be left uncut or, as in our case, cut. Although not as
luxurious or expensive as silk velvet, moquette is
quite rare because it was so heavily used, mainly
but not exclusively by the middle classes.

46 | Floral Bouquet Velvet

French, Lyon, probably manufactured by Grand
Frères, Prelle or Mathevon et Bouvard, c1874
133 × 72 cm (52 × 28 in)
Silk ciselé velvet

A brilliantly coloured red silk velvet in three
hues of red. The design features an elaborate
ornamental strapwork with rinceaux with floral
sprigs and trails. There are two central motifs of
floral bouquets, one smaller than the other. The
larger bouquet is held in place by a palmette
and either side of the bouquet are two addorsed
mascarons; these features are joined by a swag of
fruit and foliage. The smaller, which is held in an
ornamental vase, is placed on top of the pinnacle
of the cartouche strapwork; beneath this strapwork
hangs a cameo of a mascaron. At either side of the
cloth is a small bouquet which is placed on a plinth,
and beneath this plinth is a diaper pattern.

The placement of the motifs is done so that the
two central floral motifs can be used either as wall
covering or as upholstery; if the fabric was used
for upholstery then the smaller register would be
fastened to the seat back with the larger register
being used for the seat cushion.

Patterns such as these were based on both
Renaissance and Baroque designs, which
became fashionable during the second half of the

nineteenth century. These fabrics were produced by all the great weaving houses of Lyon such as Prelle, Mathevon et Bouvard, Tassinari et Chatel and Grand Frères. Similar floral velvet samples are held in the Musée des Tissus in Lyon and one example is illustrated in Sano, T. (1976), p. 195.

47 | *Sirens and Sphinxes*

French, Lyon, manufactured by Tassinari et Chatel, 1874
a) 151 × 73 cm (59 ½ × 28 ¼ in) red on cream
b) 135 × 73 cm (53 × 28¼ in) burgundy on mushroom
Silk ciselé velvet

Two impressive velvets, decorated in the Louis XIV style. Two large registers that are surrounded by *rinceaux*, arabesques, ornamental grotesques, urns and strings of pearl garlands. Two addorsed sphinxes sit on an elaborate plinth which is joined by an ornamental palmette. Upon this plinth a large ornamental urn and floral bouquet are held in place with strapwork. The second register features two addorsed winged sirens placed either side of a mascaron with elaborate headdress. Above is a dome-shaped baldachin from which hang trailing pearls. The background is decorated with *rinceaux*.

Other examples of this velvet are in the Textilmuseum in Krefeld (no. 06380) illustrated in Gasthuas, R. and Schmedding , B. (1979), pl. 36 and pl. 37; and the Cooper Hewitt Museum of Design (no. 1952-149-4) illustrated in Revere McFadden, D. (1989) p. 119. There are other examples of similar velvets held at the Chicago Art Institute, the Musée des Tissus in Lyon and the Royal Ontario Museum in Canada.

The pieces are both labelled with the manufacturer numbers. Our research shows that the red and cream colourway was woven in 1874 while the other was woven in 1884 and delivered to W. B. et Cie in February 1884.

In the eighteenth and nineteenth centuries the great Lyonnais silk houses wove high-quality fabric for the aristocracy and the royal courts of Europe. Fabrics were also woven to commission for textile merchants such as Cartier et Fils, or Duplan. However, by the second half of the nineteenth century, these firms were dealing directly with private clients, or through the tradesman or architect in charge of the client's projects, showing a shift in society with the emergence of a new *grande bourgeoisie*. Among the most famous of these commissions were the Hôtel Demidov, Hôtel Cail and Hôtel la Païva. The taste at this time was for grand, opulent interiors, furnished with luscious fabrics of historically revived designs using new, improved technology to produce fine shading effects, denser warps and silk that was manipulated to astonishing effect. These and the Païva velvets (**cat no 43 and 44**) are typical examples.

| *Baroque Revival Velvet*
French, Lyon, designed and manufactured by
Lamy et Giraud for Gillow & Co of London (later to
become Waring & Gillow), 1876
360 × 55.25 cm (142 × 21 ¾ in) panel
188 × 55.25 cm (74 × 21 ¾ in) panel
228.5 × 25.5 cm (90 × 10 in) border
Silk ciselé velvet on a cannetillé silk satin ground

A panel of silk cut and uncut velvet in hues
of brown, pink and grey on a yellow ground,
depicting a repeat design of floral arrangements,
urns and cornucopia. Accompanying the piece is
a matching border of scrolling leaves and flowers.
An illustration of this piece is shown in Schoeser,
M. and Dejardin, K. (1991), p. 142. Other examples
of this velvet are in the Art Institute Chicago,
the Minneapolis Institute of Fine Art and the Los
Angeles County Museum.

The silk is inspired by Baroque period velvets
which saw a re-birth during and shortly after
the third quarter of the nineteenth century. This
re-birth was caused mainly by the increasing
numbers of wealthy Europeans and Americans who
sought Renaissance or Baroque design styles for
the houses which they built worldwide. At the end
of the nineteenth century The New York Tribune
(1892) listed a significant increase in the number
of extremely wealthy Americans who were worth
millions of dollars (Schoeser, M. and Dejardin, K.
(1991), p. 141).

Our silk was woven by the established firm
Lamy et Giraud who provided fabrics for curtain
drapes and upholstery. According to the Prelle
archives (the successors to Lamy) this cloth
was supplied to the distinguished furniture
upholsterers, Gillow & Co.

Gillow & Co was established in 1728 by Robert
Gillow in Lancaster who provided finished furniture
to both Europe and America. Gillet & Co took a
stand at the 1851 Great Exhibition and received
the Royal Warrant as cabinet makers in 1863.
They worked with many distinguished designers
including Bruce Talbert, E. W. Godwin and T. E.
Collcutt. They also produced the furniture designed
by A. W. N. Pugin for the Palace of Westminster
and the Houses of Parliament. For the contract
sector they worked on the St Pancras Hotel and
other Midland Railway hotels, eventually becoming
important contractors for projects worldwide
including America, Australia, India and Russia. By
the start of the twentieth century they had opened
a retail furniture store on Oxford Street. Keeping
up with the change in design styles they produced
furniture in the Moderne style for the ocean liners,
R.M.S. Queen Mary, Caronia and Lusitania. They
appointed Serge Chermayeff as a director and
opened a store in Paris, which was decorated under
the direction of the designer Paul Follot. In 1953 the
firm was taken over and broken up, finally closing
in 1962.

Previous Spread

49 | ***Floral Silk with Pheasants and Butterflies***

French, Lyon, manufactured by Lamy et Giraud, 1878
301 × 148 cm (118 × 58 in), each large curtain
296 × 116.5 cm (116 × 30 in), each small curtain
Brocaded silk cannetillé with contemporary
passementerie

Two pairs of spectacular curtains decorated with
pheasants, irises and other flowers, butterflies
and small birds in an array of brilliant colours on
a black ground; the edges are trimmed with floral
scroll gimp passementerie.

The firm regularly exhibited at trade shows
and exhibitions, as a consequence of which they
became known for the high quality of their product,
winning several awards. At the Paris Exposition
Universelle of 1878 this silk design won a silver gilt
medal for the firm. A sketch of part of the silk is
illustrated in the publication of this exhibition Les
Tissus, les Broderies (1879).

Lamy et Giraud were the successors to the
Lyon silk firm Lemire, Antoine Lamy and Auguste
Giraud. They bought the rights and order book of
Lemire establishing themselves as weavers, Lamy
et Giraud, in 1865. Their chief designer was Eugène
Prelle, who became a partner of the firm in 1884.
They undertook weavings of the highest quality
and became known for their outstanding brocades,
brocatelles and damasks. In 1900 they formed an
association with Romain Gautier and the firm then
became known as Lamy et Gautier. Upon the death
of Edouard Lamy in 1918 (the son of Antoine)
the firm became wholly owned by Prelle. The
firm Prelle et Cie continues to weave today.

50 | ***Violets and Ruffles of Chantilly Lace***

French, Lyon, manufactured by Tassinari et Chatel,
c1883
a) 137 × 55 cm (54 × 21 ½ in) on a beige ground
b) 121 × 55 cm (47 1/2 × 21 ½ in) on a lilac ground
not illustrated
c) 123 × 55 cm (48 1/2 × 21 ½ in)
ciselé (cut and uncut) silk velvet on satin ground

A horizontal panel decorated with two rows of
ruffles of black chantilly lace scattered with clusters
of violets in cut and uncut velvet on a satin ground.
The fabric was woven sideways with two patterns
running side by side; the cloth was then intended to
be cut down the middle and then gently pleated.
These pieces were supplied as skirting, or a valence,
to cover the legs of furniture. Victorians found the
exposure of legs whether human or furniture
distasteful and so undertook to cover them up.

In fashion, the ruffled fabrics were made in a
lighter weight silk taffeta rather than a thick silk
and linen satin, and were tiered upon the front of
skirts. A similar pattern to our fabric was commissioned by Queen Victoria from Bonnet Frères and
supplied by Bérard et Poncet in Lyon in 1861.

According to the Tassinari et Chatel archives,
no. 5375 on the attached label indicates a date
around 1883. The fabric is illustrated in Schoeser,
M. (2007) p. 110.

51 | *Tulips*

French, Alsatian, unknown designer, manufactured
by Thierry-Mieg et Cie, 1887
221 × 81 cm (88 ½ × 32 ½ in)
Roller-printed velveteen

An all-over floral printed onto velveteen, depicting
an unusual combination of colours of brown,
deep pink and cream on a turquoise ground. The
piece was manufactured by the large printing
firm Thierry-Mieg, which was based in Mulhouse,
France. An example of this fabric was identified in
the Musée de l'Impression sur Étoffes collection
no. 647 / 2/17. The cloth shows the use of aniline
dyes of red, blue and black, which were developed
in the mid-nineteenth century. The colourway
of this fabric would have appealed to the Rajput
Maharaja in whose *toshkhana* (wardrobe) this
textile was found. During the mid to later part of
the nineteenth century French and British textile
manufacturers exported a significant amount of
stock to India.

52 | *Floral Bouquet with Convolvulus Trail*
French, Lyon, manufactured by Tassinari et Chatel,
1897
390 × 164 cm (115 ½ × 64 ½ in)
Woven brocaded silk taffeta

A large panel of unused furnishing silk, the
pattern depicts a mixed floral bouquet of tulips,
roses, peonies and hydrangeas, entwined with
convolvulus, bluebells and heartsease. Woven in
subtle shades of pinks, reds, yellows and blues
on a cream ground, the cloth is an impressive
furniture fabric. The fabric has written upon it the
manufacturer's number 7510 and a further number
53395; from the production records held at Tassinari
et Chatel we have established that the fabric was
woven in 1897.

The cloth was originally designed by Jacques
Gondoin and woven in 1771 by the Lyon silk firm
Charton, by Royal command as the summer
furnishing fabric at the palace of Versaillles for
the Dauphine Marie-Antionette. It is believed
that the Empress Eugénie of France (1826–1920)
ordered the reproduction of this pattern for use in
her boudoir. Eugénie was known to have a strong
interest in the life of Marie-Antionette, and it is this
interest which sparked a re-occurring fashion for
Neo-Classical interior design during the Second
Empire. Another example of this cloth can be found
at Waddesdon Manor, where it is upholstered
onto an ornate gold screen that is attributed to the
eighteenth-century furniture maker, J. B. Tilliard.

Two panels of this silk are also held in the
Musée des Tissus in Lyon, no. 26078 and no. 26079,
along with a further re-weave of this design. The
pattern is illustrated in Arizzoli-Clémentel, P. and
Coural, J. (1988) p. 114 and de Bellaigue, G. (1974)
pp. 625–27.

53 | *Etruscan Revival*

French, Lyon, designed after Jean-Démosthène Dugourc, probably manufactured by Prelle et Cie, or Grand Frères, 1860–80
95 × 55 cm (37 ½ × 21 ½ in)
Silk lampas

This fabric reflects the strong interest in the revival of Etruscan scenes and images from antiquity. The piece has a central image of a Pompeian figure carrying a tablet, the execution and style of the figure drawing is very much in the detailed hand of the designer Dugourc. In the late eighteenth century Dugourc produced a series of designs which featured Neo-Classical elements of satyrs, Greek gods and goddesses. Another silk sample matching our piece exists at the Musée des Tissus at Lyon (DET 158), and a similar silk to ours can also be found in the archives of Tassinari et Chatel. This piece shows the image of a Pompeian woman playing the cymbals. This silk, which was woven by Pernon in 1797 for a wall covering for one of Spanish King's Charles IV residences, is also illustrated in Hartmann, S. (1980), p. 261.

The surrounding elements to the cameo figure strongly feature a cartouche shape which is filled with a medley of floral trail with palmettes and scrolls. These pattern details can be found in the publication *The Grammar of Ornament*, written by Owen Jones and first published in 1856; this book provided many designers with a wealth of design ideas. The silk also uses a combination of the new aniline dyes, which were discovered in the mid-nineteenth century. The piece uses Lyon Blue, first discovered in 1860, and fuschine (a brilliant red).

During the mid to late nineteenth century several manufacturers became interested in the work of Dugourc and re-interpreted elements from his designs. We have attributed this piece to being either by Prelle or Grand Frères because they both manufactured silks similar to our piece.

Following Spread

54 | *Directoire Revival*

French, Lyon, probably designed in the studio at Tassinari et Chatel, manufactured by Tassinari et Chatel, c1870
146 × 75 cm (57 × 29 in)
Brocaded silk repp

A distinctive seat and chair back panel, featuring for the chair back an ornamental urn on a pediment with a floral bouquet and for the seat a cartouche with a fountain with grotesques, griffins, flaming torches and floral scrollwork. Both elements are surrounded by a pale blue egg and dart border. Densely woven as a brocaded silk repp, in a combination of cream, blue and beige silks with an ink black ground, the dyes used for this piece are a mixture of both natural and the new aniline dyes. The ground silk uses the new coal tar black colour which was discovered in 1852 by a Lancashire firm and named 'Lamp Black'.

A fabric such as this could well have been produced for a papier-mâché or lacquer chair where the frame would have been painted white or cream. This style of furniture was first seen in the Directoire period (1795–99) with a re-birth being seen in the late nineteenth century. The Tassinari et Chatel archives date this silk to around 1870.

Attached to the piece is a label and written upon it is 'patron 4345 brocade 75 in black'; a smaller label states '4345 Brocade 75cm black, sage & duck egg'.

55 | *Empire Revival Chair Seat Cover*
French, Lyon, manufactured by Tassinari et Chatel,
1900–05
202 × 65 cm (70 × 25 in)
Sabre-cut silk velvet satin

A chair seat cover which has the motif for the
seat cushion, back, arm rests and front seat trim
woven in a golden silk velvet upon a turquoise
blue ground, the pattern shows a floral starburst
medallion with ornamental scrollwork surround
for the cushion. The seat back is a cameo wreath
surround with a central motif of a lyre with the
insignia of an imperial eagle and sceptre. The arm
rests and seat trim are a smaller floral medallion.

This piece is a later re-weaving of a pattern
which was originally designed and woven for
the bedroom at Compiègne for the King of Rome
between 1802 and 1805. It was also supplied in 1830
to Queen Hortense (1793–1837) for her bedroom
at her residence, the Hôtel de Beauharnais, and
can be seen in Heutte, R. (1980), p. 84. The palace
is now the residence of the German Ambassador.
Queen Hortense was the mother of Napoleon III,
and was married to Napoleon Bonaparte's brother
Louis Bonaparte, who was King of Holland.

It is possible that this piece was a re-weave for
the Hôtel de Beauharnais to replace the worn-out
cloth that decorated the furniture. We have dated
this sample via the archives of Tassinari et Chatel
from their manufacturing numbers; the piece
is labelled with several numbers, representing
each of the pattern motifs '28586, 76140' and the
manufacturer number 8965.

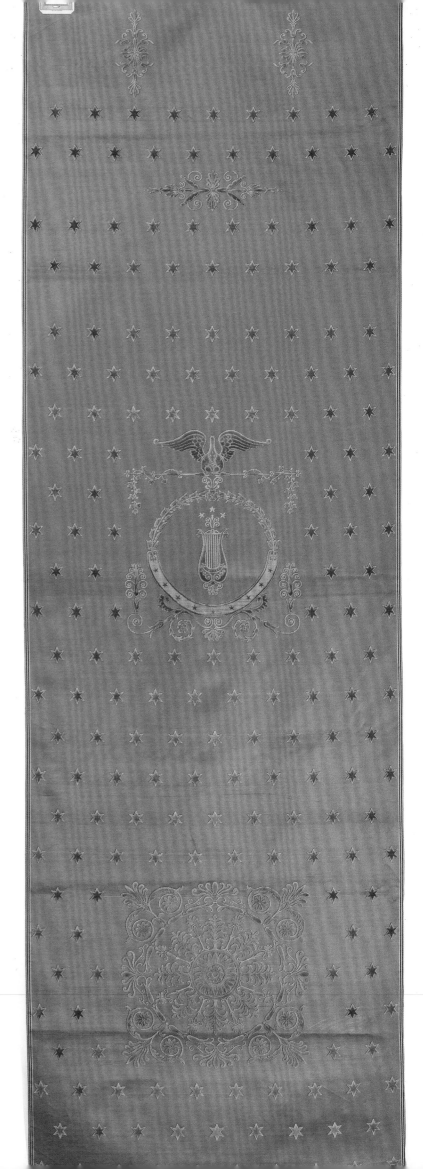

| *Jardiniere Velvet*
British, manufactured by Gainsborough Silk
Weaving Company, 1910–20
178 × 63.5 cm (70 × 25 in)
Silk ciselé (cut and uncut velvet) on satin ground

A dramatic velvet in deep purple and mustard on
a cream satin ground depicting a basket of large
stylised leaves, with a long central stem with
exuberant stylised flowers under an arcaded arch
entwined with grapes and vine leaves.

The velvet was woven by Gainsborough Silk
Weaving Company, a firm based in Sudbury in
Suffolk. The design is based on the bed hangings of
the Green Velvet Bed (c1745–50) at Hardwick Hall
in Derbyshire and is illustrated Beard, G. (1997), p.
192. Duplicate examples of the re-woven silk are
held at the Gainsborough Silk Weaving Company
archive and our sample is from the Warner family
estate. These relate in style to the Queen Anne
bed hangings woven at Spitalfields in 1714 for
Windsor Castle, now at Hampton Court, which are
illustrated in Jolly, A. (2005), p. 77, Bury, H. (1981),
p. 88, and Thornton, P. (1965), pl. 110A. This style of
velvet, referred to as Jardiniere or Garden Velvet,
originated from Genoa and was extremely popular
during the late seventeenth to the mid-eighteenth
century as furnishing fabric for upholstery and
wall decoration in the grand houses and palaces
throughout Europe.

There was a revival of the Garden Silk at the
turn of the twentieth century, which fitted well into
the Edwardian interior. Gainsborough wove this
pattern between 1910 and 1920, possibly spurned on
by the reproduction of the Windsor Castle Queen
Anne velvet produced by Warner & Sons.

Gainsborough Silk Weaving Company was
founded in 1903 by Reginald Warner, whose family
had a long association with the silk industry and
had strong connections with William Morris,
Walter Crane and Owen Jones. The firm began
by weaving historical reproductions which were
subcontracted to outworkers in surrounding
villages. In 1908 he moved to a purpose-built mill
in order to accommodate his growing number
of power looms. From such small beginnings
the mill attracted a discerning clientele. In 1912
the firm received a royal commission to weave
silk for Queen Mary's dolls' house; they finally
gained the Royal Warrant in 1980. The company
was bought out by a co-operative of employees in
2004 and today continues to weave for historical
establishments all over the world.

57 | *Different Varieties of Flowers*
British, designed by Christopher Dresser,
manufactured by Desfossé et Karth, 1879
105 × 56.5 cm (41 × 22 in) end of roll
Hand block printed wallpaper

A panel of unused wallpaper depicting rows of
clusters of stylised flowers entwined among leaf
trails printed in green, red and pinks and outlined in
gold on a dark, chocolate brown ground. The piece
represents the strong influence of the Aesthetic
movement to which Dresser was a prolific
contributor. The movement sought to reinterpret
historical periods and different cultures, creating
beautiful designs which could be manufactured
industrially. The movement began in the 1850s and
drew from contemporary literature such as Owen
Jones's *The Grammar of Ornament*, as well as
Japanese design; manufacturers were drawn to the
high quality of workmanship. Designers were also
drawn to the geometry and abstraction of the
designs which this wallpaper shows.

Dresser's theories on wallpaper design were
well received in Europe, and particularly in
England, as well as advancing the Aesthetic
look in America. By 1880 Dresser's impact on
the American wallpaper industry matched that
of William Morris. Examples of his work were
exhibited at the Paris International Exhibitions of
1867 and 1878.

Another example of this wallpaper, in a different
colour scheme, is in the Musée des Arts Décoratifs
in Paris, no. DK 7416 31A, entitled *Dessin genre
Anglais*. An example in a blue colourway is also
to be found in the Bibliothèque Forney in Paris
(number unknown), which houses the Defossé
archive. A black and yellow example is illustrated
in the publication Lyons, H. (2005), p. 283.

Defossé et Karth had many well-known
designers working for them including Christopher
Dresser, Henri Stéphany, Bruce Talbert and Owen
Jones, to name but a few. In 1855 at the Paris
Exposition Defossé presented a remarkable display
of what was termed scenic wallpapers. The firm
was determined to turn the industrial manufacture
of wallpaper into an art form. They supplied
beautifully drawn and masterfully produced hand
block printed papers, which were printed in a
dazzling array of brilliant colours.

Following Spread

58 | *Prunus Branches*
British, designed by Bruce J. Talbert, manufactured
by J. W. & C. Ward of Halifax, 1874
328 × 123 cm (129 × 48 ½ in), each curtain
Wool lampas

A large pair of curtains woven in wool with a
repeat design of small floral Prunus sprays in rose
with yellow leaves on a black ground. We have
traced the design at the Warner Textile Archive
(not numbered); notes upon the design say 'do on
Prunus loom, send to Ward, Halifax'. Prunus was
another Talbert design which was woven as a silk
tissue by Warner & Ramm.

J. W. & C. Ward were fabric manufacturers
based in Halifax, Yorkshire, established in 1868.
They wove both cotton and wool, damasks, tissues
and lampas furnishing fabrics; their biggest
market was India, in particular the Punjab region.
Many designers of the Aesthetic and Arts & Crafts
movements worked with the firm, including
Christopher Dresser, Bruce Talbert and Walter
Crane. The firm continued its production until 1911
when it was taken over by Courtaulds, another
textile manufacturer which absorbed the orders
into its own business.

59 | Hatton

British, designed by Bruce J. Talbert, manufactured
by Warner & Ramm, 1877
111 × 157.5 cm (43 × 62 in)
Silk tissue

A beautiful design which depicts an all-over
design of Prunus blossom and small insects. The
textile was produced as a silk furnishing fabric by
the manufacturer Warner & Ramm, which later
became known as Warner & Sons. The firm was
one of the most prestigious silk manufacturers in
Britain, providing the highest quality figured silks
to customers including Waring and Gillow, Liberty
& Co, Collinson & Locke, Debenham and Freebody
and several Royal households throughout Europe.
The firm regularly collaborated with leading artists
of the day. In this case the designer was Bruce
Talbert, a designer prolific in many disciplines.

The provenance and existing records for
the production of this fabric is remarkable.

Manufacturing logs held at the Warner Textile
Archive reveal that the cloth was first woven by
a master weaver, Burrows, who started to weave
the fabric on 18 May 1877; twenty-seven yards
were to be produced for an unknown customer.
A further order was placed again in December 1877,
again being woven by Burrows with an order for
fifty yards. Looking at the weaving logs it appears
that the cloth was not woven again and as such
the piece is a rare find. There is only one other
known example of this fabric and it is held at the
Warner Textile Archive, no. W1162. This piece was
exhibited in the 125th anniversary exhibition which
toured Britain from June to October 1995, no. 3. Our
piece is also illustrated in Schoeser, M. (2007) p. 94.

60 | *William Morris Collection*

British, designed by William Morris, or John Henry Dearle or Kate Faulkner, both of Morris & Co, manufactured by Morris & Co, Thomas Wardle or Stead McAlpin, samples c1875-1940
Various sizes from 206 × 97.5 cm (81 ¼ × 38 ½ in) to 55 × 25 cm (21 ¾ × 10 in)
Block-printed cottons, including five book covers, size: 65.5 × 27.5 cm (25 ¾ × 10 ¾ in)

A collection of over twenty pieces ranging from fragments to lengths, depicting twenty-two different floral designs, some inspired by Medieval decorative designs. They are printed in an array of blues, greens, reds and pinks. The collection represents a cross-section of samples which were produced by Morris & Co, or Thomas Wardle and later by Stead McAlpin. Some of these samples are very rare to find as textiles, in particular *Horned Poppy*, where it is known that this piece was produced as a wallpaper by Jeffrey & Co. Textile printing of this design is known to be of special printings only, and this design was not printed after 1900. All the samples are block printed, or are discharge printed by hand block printing. The earlier pieces have used natural dyes with the later 1940 piece being printed using coal tar dyes. The samples have come from the estate of the architect Arthur Halcrow Verstage (1875-1869). He met the elderly William Morris two years before his death and became enamoured with designs produced by Morris & Co. During his twenties and thirties he mixed with members of the Pre-Raphaelite group and was greatly inspired by the Arts & Crafts movement, and it is said that he used Morris & Co fabrics within his buildings. Verstage was the architect for Kettners Restaurant, Royalty Theatre and the Hotel Cecil.

There are many publications on William Morris and his textiles, reference is particularly made to Parry, L. (1983) and Parry, L. (2005), where most of these textiles are illustrated.

The collection includes:

1 Lodden
Designed by William Morris, hand block printed cotton, 1884.

2 Little Chintz
Designed by William Morris, hand block printed cotton, 1876, made into a book cover.

3 Tulip
Designed by William Morris, hand block printed cotton, first registered 1875.

4 Cray
Designed by William Morris, 1884, hand block printed cotton, this piece printed c1917-40.

5 Snakehead
Designed by William Morris, hand block printed cotton, c1876, made into a book cover.

6 Eyebright
Designed by William Morris, hand block printed cotton, 1883, made into a book cover.

7 Pomegranate
Designed by William Morris, hand block printed cotton, first registered 1877, made into a book cover.

8 Brer Rabbit
Designed by William Morris, hand block printed cotton, first registered 1882.

9 Borage
Designed by William Morris, 1883, hand block printed cotton.

10 Evenlode
Designed by William Morris, 1883, hand block printed cotton.

11 Horned Poppy
Designed by John Henry Dearle, hand block printed cotton, 1881.

12 Kennet
Designed by William Morris, hand block printed cotton, c1883.

13 Windrush
Designed by William Morris, hand block printed cotton, manufactured by Stead McAlpin for the Old Bleach Linen Co, 1940.

14 Medway
Designed by William Morris, hand block printed cotton, first registered 1885.

15 Strawberry Thief
   Designed by William Morris, hand block printed
   cotton, first registered 1883.
16 Indian Diaper
   Designed by William Morris, hand block printed
   cotton, c1875, made into a book cover.
17 Peony
   Designed by Kate Faulkner, 1877, hand block
   printed cotton repp, originally for Morris & Co,
   this piece for Warner & Sons, c1940.
18 Rose & Thistle
   Designed by William Morris, 1881, hand block
   printed cotton.
19 Bird & Anemone
   Designed by William Morris, hand block printed
   cotton, first registered 1881.
20 Graveney
   Designed by John Henry Dearle, 1893, hand block
   printed cotton.
21 Rose
   Designed by William Morris, hand block printed
   cotton, first registered 1883.
22 Wandle
   Designed by William Morris, hand block printed
   cotton, first registered 1884.

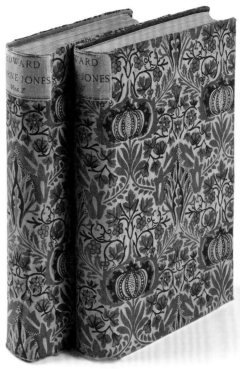

2

3

4

5 top, 6 middle, 7 bottom

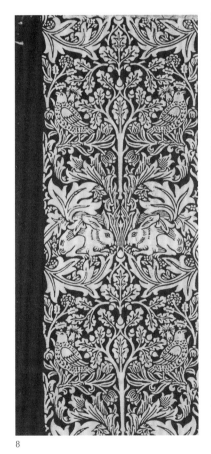

8

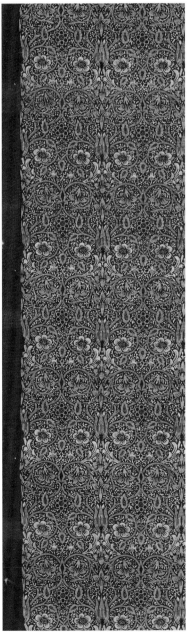

9

10

11

12

13

14

15

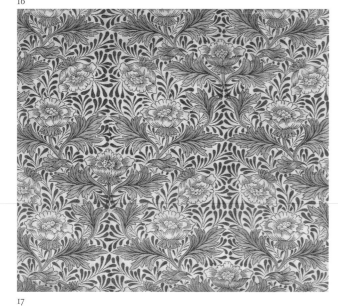

16

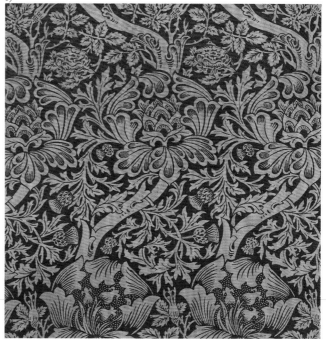

18

17

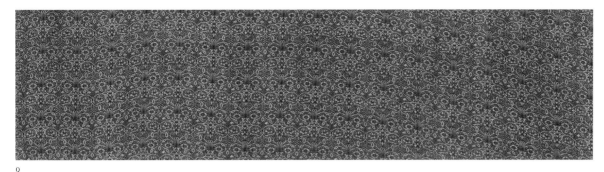

9

19

20

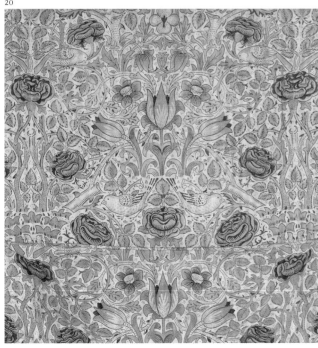

21

22

61 | Oriental Garden

British, designed by John Illingworth Kay, 1893,
manufactured in Mulhouse for Richard Stanway,
1895
224 × 71 cm (88 × 28 in)
Roller-printed velveteen

This pattern is dominated by the powerful vertical
emphasis of the tall pointed rose bushes, matched
with the swirling canopy and refined trunk of a
stylised tree. The gouache design was produced by
John Illingworth Kay, a senior designer at the Silver
Studio, who worked under the influence of Harry
Napper. The piece in true Silver Studio style does
not have a name but is numbered 1745, a number
given in systematic sequence to the production of
their designs. The studio normally left the naming
of the designs to their clients. The pattern was
originally designed to be made into wallpaper;
our research has located a watercolour design
smaller in scale at the Leicester Paint Stainers
archive, who named the piece *Oriental Garden*; the
design would have been produced as a surface-
printed wallpaper, although there is no evidence
that the design reached fruition. The design and
sale documentation for this piece is held within
the Museum of Domestic Design & Architecture
(MoDA), no. 1184.1979, and is illustrated in Turner,
M. and Ruddick, W. (1980), p. 87, and Parry, L.
(2005), p. 97.

The records at MoDA show that the pattern
was sold to Richard Stanway for £5.5s, who had
the pattern printed as a roller-printed velveteen in
1895; it was retailed through the Liberty & Co store
in both London and Paris. It may also have been
Stanway who sent the design to the wallpaper mill
to have a matching paper produced as well.
Richard Stanway became a partner in the silk
weaving business of Warner & Ramm, seeing the
firm becoming Warner, Ramm & Stanway in 1878.
After a disagreement he left the partnership to
set up on his own, trading as a furnishing fabric
wholesaler, selling cretonnes, velveteens and
various silks. He regularly purchased designs from
significant designers such as Voysey and Godwin
as well as the Silver Studio. Stanway's business
was active from 1878 to 1906.

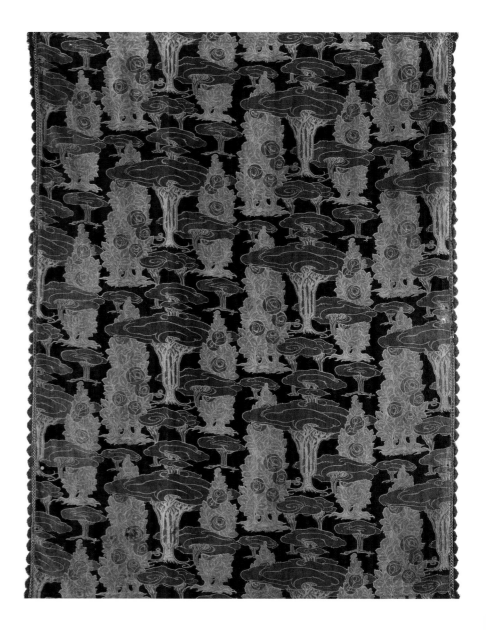

62 | Royal Burgundy

British, manufactured by Thomas Wardle & Co, for
Watt & Co, 1882
344 × 102 cm (135 × 40 in)
Hand block printed velveteen

The design of large ogivals containing stylised
pomegranates and flowers surrounded by garlands
of small hanging pears is a historical rendition of a
Renaissance style of silk velvets that were woven
in the late fifteen century. The cloth is hand block
printed in burgundy red on a light pink ground
with cream highlights. Both selvedges are present
and one of them is marked 'Wardle & Company, 71
New Bond Street'. The design was registered on
9 November 1882 with the pattern being printed
between 1882 and 1885.

During the Victorian era, there became a
fashion for the revival of Medieval and Renaissance
decorative arts. The wealthy classes had interior
room settings made which featured Gothic-inspired
stained glass, thickly carved oak furniture and
cloth which was inspired by the silks and velvets of
the fourteenth and fifteenth centuries. The Gothic
era became romanticised through the literature
of the day and the arts, particularly the paintings
produced by the Pre-Raphaelite movement. This
cloth was sold to Watt & Co, who were suppliers
of cloth to the Catholic Church and the Church of
England as well as to the secular market, and as
such they sought to retail cloth that would suit both
market sectors as this pattern would.

Thomas Wardle (1831–1909) was an innovative
textile printer and merchant of yarns and silks,
who influenced many designers of his time. He
owned three print works at Leek: Churnet which
he bought in 1875 and Hencroft which he bought
in 1872 and then leased to the printer Samuel
Tatton until 1875. The family also owned a smaller
print works called Leebrook; both the Churnet and
Hencroft works were opened under the Wardle
name in 1875. The Churnet Works was mainly used
for commercial dyeing, and the Hencroft Works
started out as a workshop where experimental
dye and print techniques were undertaken; it then
later became a full print manufacturer. From 1875
Wardle undertook to work with William Morris at
his Hencroft mill, reviving recipes for vegetable
dyes and experimenting with discharge printing,
an area that Morris was keen to develop. Wardle's
was one of a few firms which provided Morris
with some of his cloth. The firm was actively
involved with the Silk Association and the Arts &
Crafts Society; they provided the Leek Embroidery
Society with the printed silk ground cloths and
yarns for their embroidery patterns. These printed
embroidery kits were also sold through stores such
as Liberty & Co or the Wardle & Co shop based in
New Bond Street. The shop was wound up in 1888
with the Hencroft mill closing in 1908. The Wardles
did open a further mill, called Pale Meadow, based
in Shropshire, which was run under the Bernard
Wardle & Co name.

Thomas Wardle was very interested in
Islamic, Persian and Indian patterns and so
travelled extensively collecting design ideas
for his company's production. While visiting
these countries he also took the opportunity to
import silk cloth made in India, which he dyed
and printed in Leek. By the turn of the twentieth
century the company was purchasing designs
from many contemporary designers of the day
including Voysey, Lindsey Butterfield, Sidney
Mawson and E. Godwin.

Watt & Co was founded in 1874 by three
leading architects, G. F. Bodley, Thomas Garner
and George Gilbert Scott; the company at first
produced furniture, textiles and needlework of
the highest standards and quality. Their main
business for textiles was to the ecclesiastical
trade, providing copes and chasubles as well
as altar frontals and altar linen. The firm
later branched out into carpets, jewellery
and wallpaper. Their showroom and head
office was based at Baker Street in London
where it remained until 1951, then moving to
Westminster. The firm today still supplies both
church and domestic markets and is based at

63 | Chelsea Harbour, London.

Bird

British, designed by C. F. A. Voysey, manufactured
by Swaisland Printing Company for G. P. & J. Baker,
c1893
224 × 71 cm (88 × 28 in)
Hand block printed velveteen

A pattern which features a bird among a large
scrolling leaf and flower trail, the style of the
drawing is very much in the Aesthetic and Art
Nouveau style, which Voysey was famous for. The
cloth was intended to be block printed onto linen;
however, company records reveal that the pattern
was manufactured as a block-printed velveteen,
in three colourways of blue, red and olive (green).
The company retailed the cloth through the store
Liberty & Co, which marketed it as furnishing
fabric for upholstery and drapes. The watercolour
design by Voysey was given by the firm to the
Victoria & Albert Museum, no. E59-1961. The
watercolour and fabric have been shown in several
exhibitions including *Arts & Crafts Textiles*, October
1999, cat. no. 35, and the G. P. & J. Baker 100th
anniversary exhibition held at the V & A from May
until October 1984, cat. no. 96. Illustrations of the
watercolour design are shown in Parry, L. and
Rothestien, N. (1980), pp. 57 and 80. This striking
pattern has also been illustrated in MacCarthy, F.
(1972), p. 137, and in Levi, P. (1984), p. 23.

The firm G. P. & J. Baker began its life by the
arrival of George Baker in Constantinople in 1847; a
natural born business man, he began importing
linens to Turkey, supplying the ladies of the British
Embassy with curtaining and domestic fabrics.
Baker's children also worked for the firm, with
George Percival and James (Jim) taking up posts as
agents to their father's Constantinople firm. In 1878
George and George Percival travelled to Persia and it
was here that they saw the potential for exporting
carpets and embroideries to Britain. In 1884 the firm
G. P. & J. Baker was formed through a gift of £5500
from their father. The firm started importing oriental
carpets and printed textiles and acted as buying and
selling agents for Eastern firms; it also sold printed
cloth which was produced in Britain. The firm had a
long association with the manufacturing outfit
Swaisland Printing Company based in Crayford in
Kent; they eventually purchased the mill from the
liquidator in 1893. In 1907 the firm became a public
limited company. The firm continued to sell fabrics
but during the mid-twentieth century onwards they
concentrated solely on their domestic printed
furnishing fabric ranges. In 1964, they were
purchased by Parkertex, the textile division of
Parker Knoll, which in turn sold both G. P. & J. Baker
and Parkertex to the American textile wholesaler
firm Kravat Inc in 2001.

64 | *Tulip*

British, unknown designer, manufactured by
Turnbull & Stockdale, for Arthur Sanderson 1897–
1902
270 × 74 cm (106 × 29 in)
Hand block printed velveteen

A length of yellow and green printed velveteen,
featuring an all-over tulip image with long
scrolling leaves with sprigs of mallow marsh
interspersed between the tulip stems. The cloth
was manufactured by the established print
manufacturer Turnbull & Stockdale, who also
produced a variety of very similar patterns, all
featuring long-stemmed tulips. Some of these
patterns were designed by the distinguished
designer F. Day Lewis who worked for Turnbull as
well as publishing books on textiles.

From our research, we have found that
similar patterns were retailed by the firm Arthur
Sanderson, which acted as an agent for Turnbull
& Stockdale, stocking their cloths. Although we
have not found this exact piece in the Sanderson
archive, we have assumed from the other existing
samples that this piece would have been retailed
by them as well.

Between 1897 and 1902 there was a glut of tulip
designs with long flowing stems; the Silver Studio
produced similar pieces in 1897 and we have found
from record books stored at the National Archives
in London that the manufacturers Newman Smith
and Newman, C. B. Hemingway & Sons, G. P. &
J. Baker and Thomas Wardle all produced very
similar designs up to 1902.

Turnbull & Stockdale was started in 1881 and
was originally based in Ramsbottom in Lancashire.
At first the company supplied an array of services
including bleaching, piece dyeing and the finishing
of cloth such as chintzing. They also hand block
printed furnishing cloth, for the wholesaler
merchant trade, and later introduced hand screen
printing in the 1940s, moving to rotary printing in
the 1960s. From the late 1940s they sold a retail
line of cloth through the name *Rosebank Fabrics*;
this line was stocked by Arthur Sanderson until
the 1970s. The firm Turnbull & Stockdale continued
trading until the mid-1950s where the directorship
passed to Edward Turnbull, and the firm became E.
Turnbull; Edward's son Paul later joined the firm in
the late 1980s with the firm changing to E. Turnbull
& Son. In 2004 the manufacturing side of the firm
moved to Thailand and formed an association
with the fabric wholesaler and manufacturer Jim
Thompson Ltd, becoming Turnbull Thompson
Ltd. It continues to provide the trade with quality
printed furnishing cloth whether screen printed or
hand block printed.

65 | Vineyard

British, designed by Edmund Hunter for St
Edmundsbury Weaving Works, manufactured at
Haslemere, 1903
95.5 × 68 cm (37 × 27 ins)
Cotton and wool tapestry

Woven in wool and cotton the design depicts a
grapevine within an architectural border; the
design seems to be inspired by an earlier design
called *Vine* designed by John Henry Dearle and
produced by Morris & Co in 1890. *Vine* is illustrated
in Parry, L. (1983), p. 159.

Vineyard was first produced as an orphrey for
the altar frontal of St Pauls Cathedral in 1902; it
then finally became a repeated design across the
width of the cloth in 1903 when it was woven as
a tapestry cloth in colours of green, red and blue
on a dark brown ground. It was first exhibited as
a tapestry hanging at the Arts & Crafts Society
exhibition held in London and at the Clarion Guild
of Handicrafts in Chester in 1903. This piece is the
kept archival sample from the tapestry weaving
of 1903 and is from the estate of Edmund and Alec
Hunter.

The pattern had a long life span and was woven
as a silk tissue as well as in cotton and viscut mix.
The cloth was sold as a stock range item through
the St Edmundsbury Weaving Works. The silk
tissue of this design was further exhibited in the
Arts & Crafts Society exhibition of 1912. *Vineyard*
was advertised as being suitable for ecclesiastical
use and as a consequence was advertised through
religious magazines such as the Church of
England *Circular* and through brochures printed
by the 'Order of the Golden Dawn', an occult
debating occult society that had within its circle
many established artists, writers and thinkers,
including Bernard Shaw, Dr Anna Kingsford (an
early suffragette who fought for women's rights),
the actress Florence Farr, the Irish revolutionary
Maud Gonne and the author William Butler Yeats.
Examples of *Vineyard* can be seen in Parry, L.
(2005), p. 91, and *The Digest: Church of England
News* (1916), p. 14.

66 | **Pinegrove**
British, designed by Edmund Hunter for St
Edmundsbury Weaving Works, manufactured at
Halsemere, c1903
102 × 135 cm (40 × 53 in)
Silk tissue

A stylised design, it depicts mythological and
heraldic beasts throughout long clumps of grass.
Unlike Hunter's other patterns there is a looser
drawn style to this design showing the animals as
if moving, rather than as if they were in a heraldic
stance where they would be placed in stiff poses.
The Edmund Hunter diary containing notes and
press cuttings, dates this design to being produced
between 1903 and 1904. Hunter wove the pattern as
a tapestry weave, as well as a silk tissue and also
as a silk and cotton tissue with the added element
of aluminium threads in the weft. An illustration
of the rule paper is featured in the publication
Murphy, W. S. (1910), p. 126, stating that the design
was to be produced as a tapestry weave.

The fabric was intended to be used as domestic
interior fabrics such as curtains, or as dresses
and coat linings. Burberry and Harvey Nichols
commissioned Hunter to produce designs which
could be used for coat linings or vesting materials.
The fabric is a woven silk and silk floss dress fabric
in subtle shades of green and cream, and has come
from the estate of Edmund and Alec Hunter.

Previous and following Spread

67a,b | **The Path**

British, designed by Edmund Hunter for St Edmundsbury Weaving Works, manufactured at Haslemere, 1904

a) 292 × 139 cm (115 × 54 ¾ in), imbeline cotton tissue

b) 86.5 × 86.5 cm (34 × 34 in), cotton tissue as a scarf

Based on studies undertaken by Hunter from the tapestries of *La Dame à la Licorne* (Cluny Museum, Paris), the design depicts a *millefleurs* path snaking its way along the length of the cloth; at several junctions there are animals – a fox, unicorn, dog and ram – alongside mythological animals – a griffin and unicorn. All are positioned in heraldic stature – rampant, segreant and salient – alongside a heraldic five-petaled rose.

Family records show that the pattern was first woven as a silk scarf and was given as a gift in 1904 to Dorothea, Hunter's wife. She records in her diary that she was overwhelmed by its beauty and of the happy time that she had with her husband while visiting the Cluny Museum in Paris. The cloth was also woven with a mixture of silk and metallic yarns and was intended for dress wear. From 1916 the cloth was produced as a cotton mix which was to be used for the domestic interior. The example (**cat no 67a**) was exhibited at the 1916 Arts & Crafts Exhibition. The interior piece was advertised in the *The Studio Yearbook of Decorative Art* (1917), p. 114, alongside cloth produced by Morris & Co, and the article suggests that such a design would be good to be placed alongside dark oak furniture. From 1927 to 1931 the pattern transferred to Edinburgh Weavers where it continued to be made as a furnishing fabric. The two fabric pieces, one for apparel and one for domestic wear, have come from the estate of Edmund and Alec Hunter.

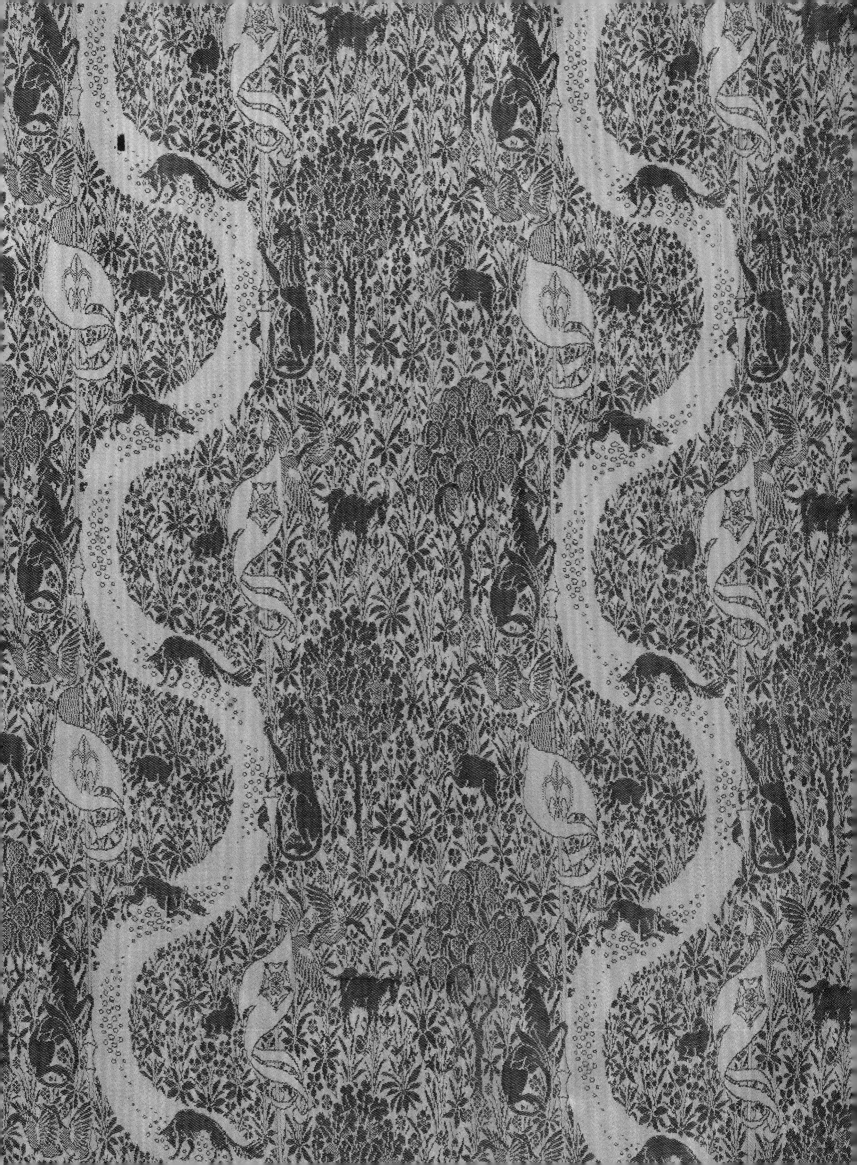

Scottish, designed by the in-house studio of Dewar & Sons, manufactured by Dewar & Sons, c1856
559 × 282 cm (220 × 111 in)
Linen and silk damask

A finely woven silk and linen damask table cloth, which was woven to commemorate the ending of the Crimean War.

The Crimean War began in 1853 and ended with the Treaty of Paris in 1856. It was fought by the allied forces of Great Britain, France and Ottoman Turkey, against Russia, which was under the rule of Czar Nicholas I. The war was started to try and curb Russia's intended expansion, which aimed to annex a chunk of the Ottoman empire which was in decline, and thus take control of the Black Sea. Sardinia later joined the Allies in 1855, for it feared being overthrown by Russia.

Lord Palmerston, the British Prime Minister, was against going to war, but public opinion, fuelled by the recent emergence of a popular press (far more people had access to education than ever before, and thus could read, and mechanised printing made a great difference) was persuaded to act. In both human and economic terms, the war cost dearly, but Russian expansion was contained.

All the important figures from the allied forces are depicted in the table cover, as are the major battles, the tugra of the Turkish Sultan and various other Imperial and Royal insignia.

1 Lyons, Admiral, Second-in-command of the fleet.
2 Cambridge, Duke of, General-in-command of the Guards Highland Brigade, fought at Alma and Balaclava.
3 Queen Victoria and Prince Albert.
4 Raglan, Lord, Commander-in-chief of the British forces.
5 Arnaud (St Arnaud), Marshal, Commander-in-chief of the French forces.
6 Florence Nightingale, who revolutionised nursing, could be described as an important feminist.
7 Bosquet, General, fought at Alma, said of the disastrous Charge of the Light Brigade, 'C'est magnificiqué mais ce n'est pas la guerre'.
8 Victor Emmanuel II, King of Italy, responsible for sending the Sardinian troops.
9 La Marmora.
10 Cardigan, Lord, fought at Alma and Balaclava.
11 Bruat.
12 Prince Napoleon, fought at Alma.
13 Napoleon III, Emperor of France (nephew of the great Napoleon).
14 Empress Eugénie (of France).
15 Simpson.
16 Pelissier.
17 Evans, commander of the British 2nd division, fought at Alma.
18 Williams.
19 Abdul Medjid, Ottoman, Sultan of Turkey.
20 Omar Pasha, Commander of the Turkish troops.
21 Canrobert, General, fought at Alma.
22 Campbell, Sir Colin, Commander of the 3rd Highland regiment.
23 'Protecit Sevastapol' 1855. During this long seige, the Czar apparently said 'I rely on my two generals, January and February'.

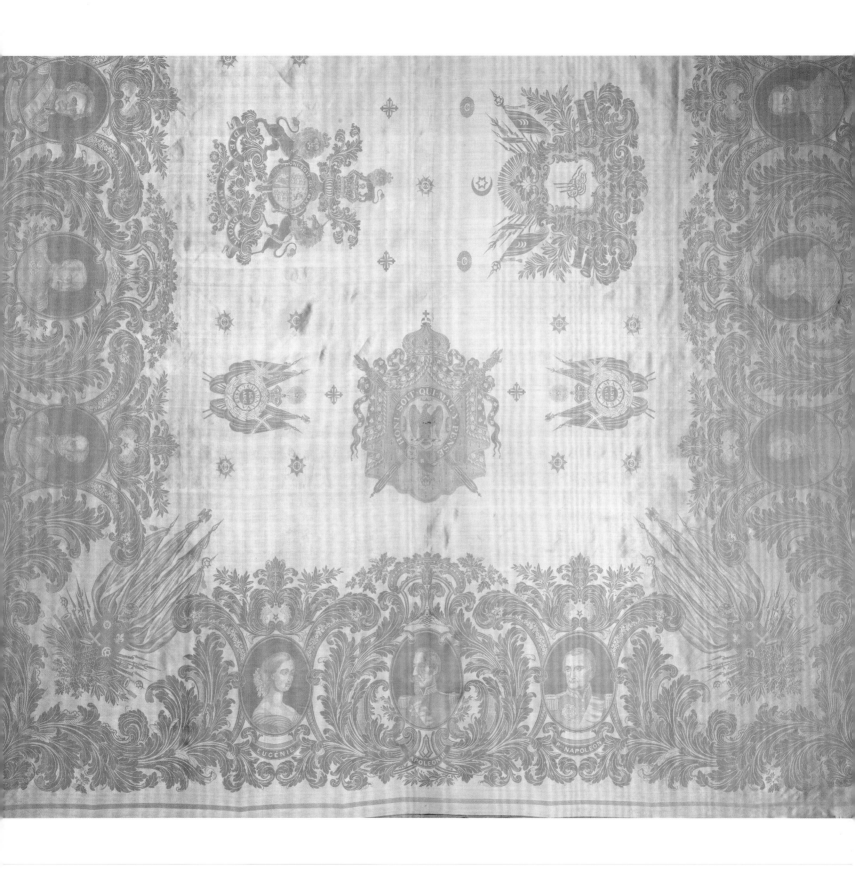

Biographies

Joseph Bourne
1740–1808

A designer who worked for many Lyon manufacturers, most of whom belonged to the *Grande Fabrique*, he is described as a shy and quiet man, who was also an accomplished still life painter. Once the Revolution came he found it hard to find work and so relied on his paintings for an income. Towards the end of his life he provided shawl designs to several Alsatian printers.

John Henry Dearle
1860–1932

Dearle began his career in 1878 as an assistant at the Morris & Co shop on Oxford Street; his talent was spotted by William Morris who trained him as a tapestry weaver and designer. He slowly worked his way up the ranks of the company becoming the firm's chief designer in 1890, working on textile designs for printed, woven and embroidered carpets, as well as tapestries and wallpapers. After Morris's death he became art director for Morris & Co.

Christopher Dresser
1834–1904

Dresser was one of the most radical designers of the Aesthetic period; he was prolific in producing well-designed objects which were to be produced by manufacturers. These items were aimed at not just the wealthy but also the mass populace. He began his career as a botanist, writing several books on the subject, but he never gained any accolade for his work. By the 1860s he was established as a leading designer of ceramics, wallpapers, metalwork, furniture, cast iron work and textiles. Working for many manufacturers including, for textiles, Warner & Sons, J. W. & C. Ward of Halifax, Barlow & Jones, Thomas Wardle, Stead McAlpin, Turnbull & Stockdale. For wallpaper, he supplied Jeffery & Co, John Perry, Desfossé et Karth and Zuber et Cie. Dresser also worked closely with retailers such as Liberty & Co and Tiffany & Co. By the end of the nineteenth century he was known for being a world authority on Japanese art having visited the country for inspiration. In 1876 he founded Dresser & Holme, importing Japanese wares.

Jean-Démosthène Dugourc
1749–1825

The only son of François Dugourc, who was controller to the household of the Duc d'Orléans, he was a gifted artist and developed his artistic training under Charles-Germain de Saint-Aubin. The son of a wealthy family he undertook to travel Europe on a Grand Tour between 1764 and 1765; this is where he established his passion and future inspiration for classical antiquity. Returning to France he worked, together with Bélanger and Georges Jacob, on the interiors of the château of Bagatelle, as well as for a glittering private clientele that included the Duc d'Aumont for the chateau Brunoy and the Duchesse de Mazarin, creating interiors in the late-eighteenth-century Etruscan style. His work linked him with European Royal Court circles and clients including Catherine II of Russia, the Spanish Royal Court and Gustav III of Sweden. In 1784 he became *Dessinateur de la Garde-Meuble*. He designed furniture for the Chambre des Bains in the château de Compiègne and a jewel cabinet for Marie-Antoinette. In 1816 he was reappointed by the *Garde-Meuble* as architect *royale*.

John Illingworth Kay
1870–1950

As a designer, he was at first based at the Silver Studio, producing designs for printed and woven textiles as well as wallpaper and graphic work for signs and book covers. In 1900 he left to become production manager of the stencilling department for the wallpaper firm Essex & Co. It appears that the firm allowed him to freelance for he provided designs to G. P. & J. Baker, Arthur Sanderson, Vanoutryve et Cie, Morton Sundour, Grafton and Liberty. In 1922 he left Essex & Co to teach part-time at the Central School of Arts & Crafts; the rest of his time was spent painting, and he became an accomplished watercolourist exhibiting at the Royal Academy.

Jacques-Louis de la Hamayde de Saint-Ange
1780–1860

Saint-Ange began his career as an apprentice architect, at first working for Antione Vaudoyer; he then moved to the architecture and interior design practice of Percier & Fontaine. While with Percier & Fontaine he continued his studies in architecture, and after graduating he became employed by the architect Alexandre de Gisors. Through his work he met Alexandre Brongniart the influential architect who designed and built for Emperor Napoleon the Paris Bourse, (the Parisian Stock Exchange) and the cemetery Père Lachaise; he also rebuilt and lived at the Hôtel de Monaco. Brongniart introduced Saint-Ange to the *Garde-Meuble* and at the age of twenty he worked for *Le Mobilier Impériale* the Royal Court, being named *inspector Le Mobilier Impériale* in 1806. He provided many designs for the *Garde-Meuble* of Napoleon Bonaparte, Louis XVIII and Charles X, and from 1808 Saint-Ange had a long collaboration with the manufacturer Beauvis. He produced designs for upholstery which were to be produced as either silk or tapestry fabrics for many of the royal palaces including Saint Cloud, the Tuileries, the Louvre, Monte Cavallo, Fontainebleau, Trianon and Compiègne. In 1816 he became *Dessinateur de la Garde-Meuble de la Couronne*. Among his most noted designs are the blue velvet and gold patterning fabrics intended for the bed chamber of King Louis XVIII at the Tuileries Palace. During the reign of Louis Philippe 1830–48 he produced designs for the porcelain factory Sèvres.

Edmund Hunter
1866–1937
Hunter was an apprentice to the commercial design firm Silver Studio; he left to form his own company in 1901, a bespoke weaving firm called St Edmundsbury Weaving Works, based at Haslemere in Hampshire. As the firm expanded and power-loom weaving became necessary he moved the firm to Letchworth in Cambridgeshire. Later on his son Alec joined him to help take on the mantle of the firm.

Kate Faulkner
c1841–1898
Faulkner started her working life producing tile paintings and then through her brother Charles she met Morris and began a long working career within the studio of Morris & Co, providing designs for wallpapers, textiles and tiles. Her brother, Charles Faulkner, was one of the founders of the firm Morris, Marshall, Faulkner and Company. Her sister Lucy was also a designer and with her brother's financial support to the firm the Faulkners became key individuals in the Arts & Crafts movement.

Philippe de Lasalle
1723–1804
Philipe de Lasalle was one of the leading silk designers and entrepreneurs of the eighteenth century, providing silk designs for the Lyon silk industry, particularly those firms belonging to the *Grande Fabrique*. He lived mainly in Lyon, but had a wide social and professional circle of acquaintances around Europe and into Russia, providing weaving designs for the Royal Courts of Catherine II of Russia and Louis XVI of France. His entrepreneurial nature is such that he was also a teacher of design, and inventor improving the technology of weaving. His design repertoire was not just for furnishing fabrics but also for fashion,

with the cloths being priced for the wealthy end of the market. Throughout his working life his business opportunities rotated from designer to wholesaler merchant, to manufacturer wholesaler. The ransacking of the 1793 Revolution hit Lasalle hard, seeing him lose his looms, designs and home, and yet within eight years he was able to rebuild his business. Lasalle was clever at anticipating the market for his silks, he had drive and determination and was ready to experiment in order to achieve his goals.

Arthur Martin Studio
c1860–c1914
The studio based in Paris provided many European manufacturers with elaborate woven designs from the mid-nineteenth century onwards. It appears that the firm ceased to exist around the start of the World War I, c1914. Designs by the firm can be found in the archives of many Lyonnais and British firms, including Warner & Sons, Grand Frères, Tassinari et Chatel and Prelle.

William Morris
1834–1896
The founder of the Arts & Crafts movement, Morris was not only a designer of textiles, wallpaper and the decorative arts but was an artist, writer of poetry and fiction and a pioneer of the socialist movement in Britain. He eschewed the industrial manufacture of goods, favouring the hand-crafted approach, working closely with firms that favoured the craft-based approach. In 1875 he founded the company Morris & Co, which produced embroideries, tapestries, carpets and woven and printed textiles; all the wares were sold through the shops based in Oxford Street and Hanover Square. In 1881 he set up the Merton Abbey Print Works, which produced the cloth for the firm.

Louis Roux
Dates unknown
A freelance designer based in Lyon, he provided expertise for producing the cloth as well as designing the pattern. He appears to have worked for most of the companies attached to the *Grande Fabrique* including Tassinari et Chatel and Prelle.

Bruce Talbert
1838–1881
Bruce Talbert was a central figure in the Aesthetic movement, and a designer who is regarded as one of the foremost designers of interiors, pioneering the role of the nineteenth-century designer whereby they worked with both industrial

manufacturers as well as specialist makers.
Talbert trained as a woodcarver and architect,
moving on to furniture design by the early 1860s.
He worked for many prestigious firms including
J. G. Crace, Gillows and Smith & Son of Dundee.
Talbert provided illustrated graphic work for
the *Illustrated London News* as well as furniture,
textiles, wallpaper, stained glass, metalwork
and ceramic tiles. At the 1878 Paris International
Exhibition he was awarded the gold medal for his
Aesthetic pattern the *Sunflower.* His design work
was reproduced in many publications and was
admired throughout the world, particularly in the
United States.

Eugène Violett-Le-Duc
1814–1879
A French architect and designer who was born
into a wealthy Parisian family, his love for the
Medieval decorative arts and architecture came
from a Grand Tour he undertook in 1836. In 1840
he gained his first important commission, which
was the restoration of La Madeleine at Vézelay,
having previously worked as an inspector at
Sainte Chapelle. He is known mainly for restoring
ecclesiastical buildings such as Notre Dame, which
he undertook in 1840. However, in 1857 he was
commanded by Napoleon II to rebuild the ruined
castle at Pierrefonds, later gaining the commission
for the interior decoration of the castle. Between
1858 and 1868 he published the ten-volume
*Dictionnaire raisonné de l'architecture Française
du XI au XVI siècle*. These volumes provided many
a manufacturer with design inspiration for their
products. In 1873 he wrote and illustrated *Histoire
d'une Maison*, which later became an inspiration
for the twentieth-century architect Frank Lloyd
Wright. Towards the end of his life he devoted his
time to writing.

C. F. A. Voysey
Charles Frederick Annesley
1857–1941
Voysey trained as an architect and designer. He
was a major influence on the architectural and
decorative art scene at the end of the nineteenth
century and in the early twentieth century. He set
up his own studio in 1882 and began to produce
designs for firms in the furnishing industry
including G. P. & J. Baker, A. H. Lee, Stead McAlpin,
Warner & Sons and Templeton. His work was also
sought by the French industry as his 'hand' worked
well with the continental Art Nouveau style.

Bibliography

Abbott, J. and Rice, E. (1997) *Designing Camelot: The Kennedy White House Restoration*, John Wiley & Sons Inc, New York.

Alcouffe, D. (1991) *Un âge d'or des arts décoratifs 1814-1848*, Galeries Nationales du Grand Palais, Paris.

Anon (1984), *Dessins du XVIe au XIXe siècle de la collection, du Musée des Arts Décoratifs de Lyon: décembre 1984-mas 1985, Salle d'exposition du Musée historique des tissus*, Musée Historique des Tissus, Lyon.

Arizzoli-Clémentel, P. (1990) *The Textile Museum*, Éditions Lyonnaises, Lyon.

Arizzoli-Clémentel, P. and Baulez, C. (1990) 'De Dugourc à Pernon: Nouvelles Acquistions Graphiques pour les Musées' in *Les Dossiers du Musée des Tissus*, December 1990-91 no. 3, Lyon.

Arizzoli-Clémentel, P. and Coural, J. (1988) *Soieries de Lyon: Commandes Royales au XVIIIe Siècle (1730-1800)*, Musée de la Chambre de Commerce et d'Industrie de Lyon, Lyon.

L'Art de la soie Prelle - 1752-2002, Musee Carnavalet, Paris 2002-03, no. 184.

Bais, Th. (1879) *Exposition Universelle Les Tissus et Les Broderies*, Librairie Centrale, Paris.

Beard, G. (1997) *Upholsterers and Interior Furnishing in England, 1530-1840*, Bard Graduate Center and Yale University Press, New Haven and London.

Bellaigue, de, G. (1974) *Furniture, Clocks and Gilt Bronzes: The James A de Rothschild Collection at Waddesdon Manor*, Fribourg in association with The National Trust, London.

Benoît, J. (2005) *Napoléon et Versailles*, Édition de la Réunion des Musées Nationaux, Paris.

Biver, P. (comte) (1933) *Historie du Chateau de Bellevue*, A Paris Librairie et Gabriel Enualt, Paris.

Blazy, G. (1998) *Musée des Tissus de Lyon, Guide des collections*, Éditions Lyonnaises, D'Art et D'Histoire, Lyon.

Bouzard, M. (1999) *La soierie Lyonnaise du XVIII au XX siècle*, Éditions Lyonnaises and D'Art et D'Histoire, Lyon.

Bury, H. (1981) *A Choice of Design: 1850-1970 Fabrics by Warner & Sons Ltd*, Purley Press, London.

Calavas, A. (1905) *Art Industrie Musée Historique Tissus de Lyon: Chois de Soieries*, Librairie des Arts Décoratifs, Paris.

Chavance, R. (c1950) *Documents et Modèles, Tissus Directoire et Empire*, Librairie Centrale des Beaux Arts, Paris.

Cleveland Museum Bulletin (1954) Vol. XLI, June 1954, Cleveland Museum, Ohio.

Coste, P. (1839) *Architecture Arabe ou monuments du Kaire mesurés et dessinés de 1818 à 1826*, de Firmin Didot Frères et Compagnie, Paris.

Coste, P. (1867) *Monuments, Modernes de la Perse, mesurés, dessines et décrits par Pascal Coste, Publiés par ordre de son excellence le ministrie de la masion d'empereur et beaux arts*, A Morel, Paris.

Coste, P. (1998) *Toutes les Égypte*, Bibliothèque Municipale de Marseille, Marseille (reprint).

Coural, C. (2002a) 'Le Consulat et L'Empire un, Age D'Or Inégalé' in *Dossier de L'Art Hors Série de L'Objet D'Art, no. 92, Les Grandes Heures de la Soierie Lyonnaise*, Éditions Fanton, Paris.

Coural, C. (2002b) 'La Restauration et la Monarchie de Juillet, D'un Empire a l'autre' in *Dossier de L'Art Hors Série de L'Objet D'Art, no. 92, Les Grandes Heures de la Soierie Lyonnaise*, Éditions Fanton, Paris.

Coural, J. (1980) *Paris, Mobilier National Soieries Empire*, Éditions de la Réunion des Musées Nationaux, Paris.

Decloux and Doury (1865) *L'Histoire Archéologique, Descriptive et Graphique de la Sainte Chapelle du Palais*, A Morel, Paris.

Downing, A. J. (1861) *The Architecture of Country Houses: Including designs for cottages, farm houses and villas*, Appleton, New York.

Dumonthier, E. (1909a) *Mobilier National, Étoffes d'ameublement de l'époque Napoléonienne*, Schmid, Paris.

Dumonthier, E. (1909b) *Les plus beaux meubles des ministères et administrations publiques*, Morance, Paris.

Dumonthier, E. (1909c) *Château de la Maison; textile historique et descriptif, ornée de 100 planches en heliotypie, donnaut plus de 200 documents dessinés specialement pour la famille impériale par Percier et Fontaine*, Co Foulard, Paris.

Dumonthier, E. (1921) *Les Sièges de Jacob Frères: Epoques du Directoire et du Consulat*, Mobilier National France, Paris.

Feulner, A. (1927) *Kunstgeschichte des Möbels, Seit dem Altertum*, Propyläen-Verlag, Berlin.

Flemming, E. (1928) *Encyclopaedia of Textiles: from Earliest Times to the Beginning of the 19th Century*, Ernest Benn, London and Berlin.

Frégnac, C. and Andrews, W. (1977) *The Great Houses of Paris*, Vendome Press, New York and Paris.

Galloway, F. (1997) *Arts & Crafts Textiles in Britain*, The Fine Art Society in association with Francesca Galloway, London.

Gasthaus, R. and Schmedding, B. (1979) *Samte*

Velvets Velours: Das Textilemuseum Krefeld zu Gast beider Girmes-Werke Aktiengesellschaft, Odet: Girmes-Werke Aktiengesellschaft, Krefled.

Gaudry, E. (1982) *Soieries de Lyon - Commandes Imperiales - Collections du Mobilier national Musée historique des Tissus*, Musée Historique des Tissus, Lyon.

Girault de Pragney, J. P. (1832) *Impressions de Grenade et l'Alhambra*, A. Hauser, Paris

Girault de Pragney, J. P. (1836-39) *Monuments, Arabes et Moresques de Cordoue Sèville et Granade: dessinés et mesurés en 1832 et 1833*, A. Hauser, Paris

Girault de Pragney, J. P. (1842) *Choix d'ornements Moresques de l'Alhambra: Monuments Arabes et Moresques de Cordoue Sèville et Grenade*, A. Hauser, Paris.

Godart, J. (1899) *L'Ouvrier en soie-monographie du Tisseur Lyonnais étude historique, économique et sociale*, Bernoux & Cumin; Arthur Rousseau, Lyon and Paris.

Goodale, E. (Sir) (1971) *Weaving and the Warners 1870-1970*, F. Lewis, Leigh on Sea.

Gruber, A. (1985) *Grotesken - Ein Ornamentstil in Textilien des 16-19 Jahrhunderts*, Abegg-Stiftung, Riggisberg.

Gruber, A. (ed.) (1994) *L'art décoratif en Europe - du Neoclassicism à l'Art Déco*, Citadelles & Mazenod, Paris.

Hartmann, S. (1980) 'Fabriques et Jardins Dessinés par Jean Démosthène Dugourc dans la Collection Tassinai et Chatel à Lyon' in *Bulletin de la Société de l'Histoire de l'Art Français*, Paris.

Heutte, R. (1980) *Les Étoffes d'Ameublement*, Editions H. Vial, Dourdan.

Jolly, A. (2005) *Fürstliche Interieurs - Dekorationstextilien des 18. Jahrhunderts*, Abegg-Stiftung, Riggisberg.

Jones, O. and Goury, Jules M. (the late) (1842) *Plans, Elevations, Sections and Details of the Alhambra: taken from drawings on the spot in 1834, Vol I*, Owen Jones, London.

Jones, O. and Goury, Jules M. (the late) (1842) *Plans, Elevations, Sections and Details of the Alhambra: taken from drawings on the spot in 1834, Vol II, Details of Ornaments from the Alhambra by Owen Jones Architect*, Owen Jones, London.

Jones, O. (1856) *The Grammar of Ornament*, Day & Son, London.

Jones, O. (1865) *The Grammar of Ornament*, Bernard Quaritch, London.

Jones, O. (1868) *The Grammar of Ornament*, Bernard Quaritch, London.

Junquera, J. J. (1979) *La Decoración y el mobiliario de los palacios de Carlos IV*, Oganización Sala Editorial, Madrid.

Kraatz, A. (1988) *Dentelles / Anne Kraatz*, F. Bourin, Paris.

Lasteyrie, de, F. and Darcet, A. (1855) *L'ecclésiologie a L'Exposition, Annales Archéologiques*, tome V, P. Jamot, Paris.

LeClercq, J-P. (2004) 'Union Centrale des Arts Décoratifs Musée de la Mode et du Textile' in *La Revue des Musées de France, Revue du Louvre*, Paris, 2 April 2004.

Levi, Peta (1984) 'The Rise and Rise of the Baker Business' in *Homes and Garden*, May 1984, Conde Nast, London.

Lyons, H. (2005) *Christopher Dresser: The People's Designer 1834-1904*, The Antique Collectors' Club, Woodbridge.

MacCarthy, F. (1972) *All Things Bright and Beautiful*, Allen & Unwin, London.

Marinis, F. (1994) *Velvet: History, Techniques, Fashions*, Idea Books, Milan.

Martin, R. (1983) *Silks from the Palaces of Napoleon*, FIT, New York.

The Metropolitan Museum of Art Bulletin (1936) Vol. XXXI, April 1936, Metropolitan Museum of Art, New York.

Morand, D. (1930) *English Decorative Textiles: Their Designs & Development from the Earliest Times to the 19th Century*, John Tiranti, London.

Murphy, J. Cavanah (1813) *The Arabian Antiquities*, Cadell & Davies, London.

Murphy, W. S. (1910) *The Textile Industries: A Practical Guide to Fibres, Yarns and Fabrics, Vol. VI*, Gresham Publishing, London.

Oglesby, C. (1951) *French Provincial Decorative Art*, Charles Scribners & Sons, New York.

Palmer, D. (2007) *Letters to 13 Berkeley Square 1841-1847*, David Palmer, Rothwell.

Parker, J. et al (1964) *Decorative Art from the Samuel H. Kress Collection at the Metropolitan Museum of Art*, Phaidon for Kress Foundation, London and New York.

Parry, L. (1983) *William Morris Textiles*, Weidenfeld & Nicholson, London.

Parry, L. (2005) *Textiles of the Arts & Crafts Movement* (new edn), Thames & Hudson, London.

Parry, L. and Rothenstien, N. (1980) *From East to West: Textiles by G. P. & J. Baker*, G. P. & J. Baker & Co, High Wycombe.

Poidebard, A. and Chatel, J. (1912) *Camille Pernon: Fabricant de Soieries a Lyon 1753-1808*, Librairie Ancienne de Louis Brun, Lyon.

Praz, M. (1964) *An Illustrated History of Interior*

Decoration, From Pompeii to Art Nouveau, Thames & Hudson, London.

Prisse d'Avennes, A-C-T. E. (1885) *La Décoration Arabe*, J Savoy & Cie, Paris.

Racinet, A. (1873) *Polychromatic Ornament*, H Sotheran & Co, London.

Revere McFadden, D. (1989) *L'Art de Vivre: Decorative Arts and Design in France 1789-1989*, Vendome Press, New York.

Richardson, J. (2000) *The Courtesans: The Demi-Monde in 19th Century France*, Phoenix Press, London.

Riley, N. (2003) *The Elements of Design*, Free Press, London.

Sano, T. (1976) *Étoffes Merveilleuses du Musée Historique des Tissus, Lyon, Tome II, Soieries françaises du XIX et du XX siècle*, Gakken, Toyko.

Sano, T. (1980) *British Textile Design in the Victoria & Albert Museum, Vol III, 1850-1940*, Gakken, Tokyo.

Schober, J. (1930) *Silk and The Silk Industry* (translated by R Cuthill), Constable, London.

Schoeser, M. (2007) *Silk*, Yale University Press, New Haven and London.

Schoeser, M. and Dejardin, K. (1991) *French Textiles from 1760 to the Present*, Thames & Hudson, London.

Slavin, R. (1992) *Opulent Textiles: the Schumacher Collection*, Crown, New York.

Soria, A. (2002) 'La Suprématie Lyonnaise' in *Dossier de L'Art Hors Série de L'Objet D'Art, no. 92, Les Grandes Heures de la Soierie Lyonnaise*, Éditions Fanton, Paris.

Tassinari, B. (2005) *La Soie à Lyon: de la Grande Fabrique aux textiles du XXI siècle*, Éditions Lyonnaises d'Art et d'Histoire, Lyon.

Tassinari et Chatel (1999-2006) *Catalogue Tassinari et Chatel*, Tassinari et Chatel, Lyon.

The Digest: Church of England News (1916), The Church of England, London

The Studio (1917) *The Studio Yearbook of Decorative Art*, The Studio Ltd, New York, London, Paris.

Theunissen, A. (1934) *Meubles et sièges du XVIII Siècle; menuisiers, ébénistes,marques plans et ornementation des leurs oeuvres*, Editions 'Les Documents', Paris.

Thornton, P. (1965) *Baroque & Rococo Silks*, Yale University Press, London.

Thurman, Christa C. Mayer (1992) *Textiles in the Art Institute of Chicago*, Art Institute of Chicago, Chicago.

Tuchscherer, Jean-Michel (1987) 'Un ensemble de soieries Lyonnaises d'ameublement en Espagne' in *Bulletin du Centre International d'Etude des Textiles Anciens*, Paris.

Turner, M. and Ruddick, William (1980) *The Silver Studio Collection*, Lund Humphries, London.

Valentin, F. (2003) 'Triomphe du néo-gothique – Le néo-gothique: un phénomène parisien?' in *L'Art de la Soie, Prelle 1752-2002, des ateliers Lyonnais aux palais parisiens*, Musée Carnavalet, Paris, pp. 136-38.

Verlet, P. (1963) *Les ébénistes du XVIII Siècle Français*, Hachette, Paris.

Verzier, P. (1998) 'Les Grandes Heures de la Soierie Lyonnaise' in *L'Estampille L'Objet d'Art*, no. 327, September 1998, Les Editions Faton, Dijon.

Verzier, P. (2002) *Soies Tissées, Soies Brodées Chez L'Impératrice Joséphine*, Réunion des Musées Nationaux, Paris.

Victoria & Albert Museum (1975) *Liberty's 1875-1975: An Exhibition to Mark the Firm's Centenary*, Victoria & Albert Museum, London.

Viollet-le-Duc, E. (1858-68) *Dictionnaire raisonné de l'architecture française du XI au XVI siècle* (ten volumes), Deuxième édition, Paris.

Viollet-le-Duc, E. (1858-75) *Dictionnaire du mobilier français de l'époque carlovingienne à la Rénaissance* (six volumes) Bance, Paris.

Walton, Whitney (1992) *France at the Crystal Palace: Bourgeois Taste and Artisan Manufacture in the Nineteenth Century*, University of California Press, Los Angeles.